Make It Happen

Motivation. Meditation. Manisfestation

By Rev. Janice Chrysler

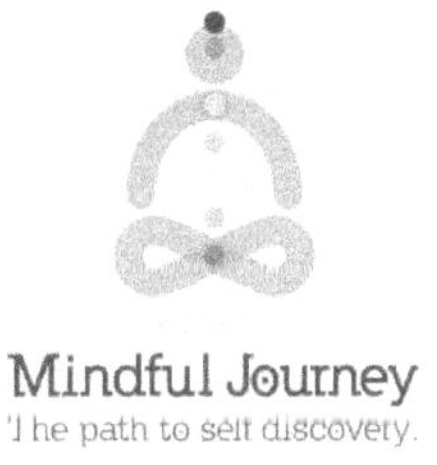

ISBN 978-0-9949831-1-4 <Book>
ISBN 978-0-9949831-1-4 <Digital>
ISBN 978-0-9949831-2-1 <Paperback>
ISBN 978-0-9949831-3-8 <Electronic Book>

Interior Design and layout by Willow Publishing
Cover design by Jenn E. Bennett, Creative Consultant
Photography by Ash Nayler, www.ashnayler.com
Editor: Dawn James
Publisher: Mindful Journey
Website: www.MindfulJourney.ca

 Printed and bound in Canada.

Dedication

With much love and gratitude I would like to dedicate this book to my husband and soul mate. Monty, you have been a constant in my life since we were eleven years old, and I am truly thankful that you have chosen to share life's journey with me. As well to my mother, who has shown and taught me more than she will ever realize. Then there are my two soul sisters, who remind me to laugh, take road trips, and simply be myself.

Thank you to all my students, clients, family, and friends, who have opened your hearts and souls to me. I know I have learned so much from you, and I will be ever grateful for your love and support. Most of all, I give thanks each day to the Divine, the angels and guides who work around me and through me. May they also be a comfort and support to you as you venture out to Make it Happen.

Table of Contents

Make It Happen

Preface.......... i

Introduction.......... v

Chapter One: Power of Your Thoughts.......... 1

Chapter Two: What Moves You?.......... 31

Chapter Three: What Do You Fear?.......... 45

Chapter Four: Mind, Body and Spirit...Bringing it all together.... 55

Chapter Five: Meditation and You.......... 67

Chapter Six: Letting Go.......... 89

Chapter Seven: Opening to Receive.......... 105

Chapter Eight:Following Your Intuition.......... 111

Chapter Nine: Stepping Out of Your Comfort Zone.......... 121

Chapter Ten: Time to Make it Happen.......... 129

About the Author.......... 133

Services by Rev. Janice Chrysler.......... 134

Mindful Journey Publishing.......... 134

Mindful Journey Meditation Series.......... 134

Preface

Like everyone else on this journey called life, I have experienced my own ups and downs, crooked passages, and what, at the time appeared to be a dead end. I have been lost, back on track, and able to climb many a tall mountain, with the guidance and assistance of many wonderful and caring people. Some of them have bravely chosen to share my trip from start to finish (*I don't plan on being done for quite some time),* while others took part for only a brief moment in time. There were times when I felt totally abandoned, and other times I felt lost in a crowd. There were times I sat in judgment of myself, where I was the lone player of a pity party, and times of great excitement over the smallest of victories of my own, or others.

It took many of life's experiences before I totally understood how much of my reality I was creating. Fortunately, I have always been a fairly positive person, looking for the good in everything. However, I struggled for a good portion of my adult life with accepting my truth, my path, and how to use my intuitive gifts. I had to learn to step out of what was dictated to me as being the *"right"* way of thinking, and behaving. It was only then that I truly began believing in myself, and following my heart. It involved, not only faith in the Divine and the Universe, but in my own ability to manifest changes in my life…and I believe I deserved that change. One thing was to understand that the answers to our biggest questions can often come in the simplest of ways.

About ten years ago, I found myself at a spiritual cross road in my life. By now I was starting to trust my intuition just a bit more, so when I felt the Universe nudge me to pick up the book by Dr. Seuss, *"Oh the Places You'll Go",* I felt compelled to read through it. I expected it was simply to cheer me up, as I had always enjoyed his books. The crazy rhymes and names intrigued me as a child, and made reading the same story over and over again as an adult, fun and exciting. I was slightly disappointed when my children no longer needed me to read to them, especially the antics of Dr. Seuss. However, this time, the words popped out at me, and my present life situation—especially when I came to the part about being in a slump—alone. It basically states you have to get yourself out of this place by yourself and it will not be easy. There will be many decisions to make, and if you don't make them, you will find yourself in a most useless place: *The Waiting Room*.

Strange but true, I then realized that was how I felt. I was always waiting for something to happen, someone to say or do something… waiting, waiting, waiting…everyone just waiting, and I waited with them. I didn't want to be stuck in this room any longer. It was then I realized that just because others were sitting around, didn't mean I had to as well!

As Dr. Seuss says, *"NO! That's not for you! Somehow you'll escape all that waiting and staying. You'll find the bright places where Boom Bands are playing."* I suppose this was the start of my realization that I did have choices, and only I could make them. I had to take responsibility for my life and start living it, manifesting what I wanted to make me happy, and discovering my purpose. That was it, I needed to find my purpose in life, and not only that, but to grab hold of it, and live it! I decided that moment was the day that I would get out of the *Waiting Room,* and create my own reality.

So my journey began. I meditated more sincerely, listened more intently, and believed in the Divine and workings of the Universe more fervently. I learned to follow my own intuition and to truly trust that there was a plan for me. All I had to do was be open to receive the answers to my questions, be aware of the signs and opportunities presented to me, and most importantly, take the leap of faith to follow those feelings. By trusting everything would work out, I quit one job and ventured into a whole new career. I decided to follow my passion in helping others and became a Reiki Master, and Certified Hypnotherapist, specializing in Past Life Regression (what I call Journey of the Soul), Spiritual Growth Facilitator, author, an ordained Metaphysical Minister, and founder of Mindful Journey. The meeting of people at just the right time, events, and opportunities, continued to blend one into another. All this confirmed that life is made up of synchronicities, if only we take the time to open our eyes and hearts to see them.

One thing I have learned is that once the journey of self-discovery and connection with the Divine begins, there is no going back. I also have learned that the trip is not without its bumps and bangs, and often the path is just wide enough for one. Friends and family cannot, or choose not to make the trip with me. So much of the learning and growing is a game that I must play by myself. By keeping my thoughts positive, and for the higher good, I will find meaning in this game of life. My purpose is to tell others about my trip, and teach them what I have learned so far. This book is part of that path; discovering the way to manifest for the Higher Good in your life.

You too have the ability to move mountains, and to make your mark in this lifetime, whether it is a giant footprint for mankind, or a single moment in time in someone's day. Face your fears, move ahead, accept what the Universe has to offer, be patient with others, and be especially kind to yourself. What are you waiting for? Let your journey begin.

Namaste

Rev. Janice

Introduction

Do you ever wonder where you are going in your life, if anywhere? Do you ask yourself: *what is my purpose to my being on this little blue planet at this moment in time?* It is not uncommon to have these questions pop into your mind from time to time. Sometimes these thoughts are only there for a brief moment, hardly noticed, like a soft summer breeze passing through. Then there are those times when your search for your purpose seems to weigh heavily on your consciousness, almost consuming your every thought and breath. What if this is your Higher Self, seeking and prompting you to explore your present situation, and begin discovering your soul's journey?

What if where you are is exactly where you are meant to be at this moment in time? What if you didn't need to know or understand every step of the way in order to fulfill your destiny? Could it be that all that is expected of you is to take one step at a time, and in this way you discover who you are, and what you are meant to do? Too often you can get caught up in the how, why, or why not of the situation, and lose sight of your purpose, and your desires. You may even forget that your reality is created within you, and what you see around you is unique to your soul's growth. By accepting that you are doing the best you can at this moment in time, and making the most of each day, you will soon find your way, and realize you have the power within to make changes through your thoughts, belief in yourself, and to manifest what you desire.

Once you are sure of your purpose, you will then be busy finding ways to make it happen! By letting go of limitations on how things should go, you will be open to receive all the countless opportunities that are presented to you. Many lessons in patience, compassion and understanding, as well as self-acceptance and self-love, are learned in this part of your journey. By accepting that there are endless possibilities all around you, and freeing your heart of past negative emotions and future worries, you are then able to allow pure potentiality to be exposed and take form. It is about having faith in those things you cannot see or fully understand, and then believing that your intuition and spiritual connection to the Divine and the Universe will guide you to where you are to go. Believing you are here for a reason at this moment in time, and trusting the Divine will give you the directions you need when you need them, will bring you through every treacherous passage.

Choices will need to be made along every step of the way. There will be times that you choose a less traveled path, and in doing so may either come to learn many personal and powerful lessons for your own evolution, or you will be the pioneer who opens up a whole new trail for others to follow. Sometimes you will travel with others for either a long time, or a short trip. Many times you will feel you are alone on this journey, which can send you on a seemingly spiral decent into the Darkness of the Soul. It is during those times that you find in the stillness of meditation and contemplation, and the strength and wisdom to continue along your path. This journey will have many ups and downs, twists and turns. Each one a new adventure to be explored and remembered. Some will bring you pleasure, and some will bring you pain, but all of them will help you to become more spiritually enlightened, if you allow the Divine's unconditional love to work through you. This love is always within and around you. You only need to find the stillness in your heart centre, and allow it to flow without effort through every cell of your being to awaken your soul's journey.

It is through this journey of self-discovery that will awaken the knowledge you are the creator of your own reality. Within your mind, body, and spirit, lies the power for you to *Make it Happen*!

Chapter One:

Power of Your Thoughts

"*A man is but the product of his thoughts what he thinks, he becomes.*" ~Mahatma Gandhi

Thoughts, had any lately?

Your mind is a wonderful tool that, if you are like the rest of the human race, you may unfortunately misuse, or worse yet, seemingly not use at times. Every single day you have between 60,000 and 80,000 thoughts moving through your mind for you to sort through. Believe it or not, it is all up to you what you will keep to use now, discard, or store for a later date. The control over how and what you think is always up to you, and that, my friend, is the key to your manifesting what you desire in your life. It is known as your free will. You choose what information you keep, and how you react to the information in the way of speech, actions, emotional, and physical reactions. Even though you may not wish to admit it, no one "*makes*" you act a certain way, or say certain things, or feel unworthy or better than everyone else. You decide how you will react to certain words, emotions, and situations. The words and actions of others may trigger a memory, which in turn will create a reaction, but in the end it is all up to you, if you choose to carry the action through. All this can happen so fast that you don't even realize it, but once you understand how this works, you begin to bring control back into your own life.

Even when you sleep, your thoughts are still active through dreaming. The thoughts are manifesting ways to create your reality. How many restless nights have you spent going over and over the day's events, or in worry about what is yet to come? What if you could learn to turn those sleepless nights into times when your mind actually sorted everything out for you, while your physical body found rest and relaxation? You most likely have already had this happen without even trying. Think about a time when upon awakening, you were able to find the solution to a problem. The old saying, *"sleep on it and things will look better in the morning,"* can take on a whole new meaning for you!

Are your thoughts your own?

It is believed that 95% of your thoughts are all repeat episodes of past events from yesterday, last year, or life times ago. They can be ideas and thought patterns that you learned as a child, came to accept through culture and religion, but perhaps were not really your own. Unless you take time to examine why you think what you do, and how you react to your own thoughts, you can easily be repeating patterns that either no longer serve you, or are contributing to your feeling stuck. No doubt if you own a car, you will change the oil so you get optimum performance from your vehicle, so why not change your thoughts so you can use the ideas you conceive, in order to help you achieve what you desire?

Have you ever found yourself repeating the same old pattern and lamenting, *"Why me? Why can't things ever go right for me?"* Guaranteed you are attempting to make changes by doing the same thing, in the same way you always have, and getting nowhere.... again! Isn't it crazy that you really think acting the same way, doing things the same way, treating others, and being treated by others the same way, is somehow magically going to create a new and exciting outcome! The following is a definition of insanity by *Albert Einstein*:

"Insanity: doing the same thing over and over again and expecting different results."

Mind you, you may have to do something a couple of times to recognize your mistake, but after awhile, if you truly want to make changes it would serve you well to step back and look at the situation as objectively as possible, then take responsibility for your part in the whole situation. Remember, you are in charge of those 60,000 to 80,000 daily thoughts running through your head! Now is the time to understand how your mind is operating, so you can begin to control your own destiny.

A Mind Divided

Since your reality and ability to manifest in your life begins with your thoughts, it is a good idea to take a brief look at how your mind works. Over the centuries there have been many discussions, theories, and controversies about what goes on in that grey matter. The main question that continues to arise is in regard to how the conscious and/or the subconscious mind works, or if they even exist at all. If you were to examine a human brain, all you would see is the physical structure. No where could you find the *"spot"* where all the thoughts are stored, but store them you do! A simple way to describe the conscious and subconscious minds is by the *"Iceberg"* analogy. The tip of the iceberg is what you can see, but it is not what sinks the ship; it is the 90% that is hiding under the water that you cannot see that does this. With your mind, it is the conscious mind that is the 10%, while the hidden subconscious mind is the other 90%. So, how do they work?

Subconscious Mind

Think of this part of your mind as a file on your computer hard drive. It is there collecting data, memories, your reactions to past situations, all the information that was given to you as a child, and through life experiences. It stores, like a computer file, without judgment as to whether the information is right or wrong, but simply tucks it away so that you can retrieve it at a later date. In the same way the computer's operating system automatically runs the computer program, your subconscious mind also runs your bodily functions. You don't have to consciously think about breathing, walking, how to talk, keep your heart beating, or digest your food. All these types of thoughts will happen in milliseconds. It takes the information, and automatically will provide you with actions and reactions, based on the stored data that you have accumulated over your life time(s). It is not rigid or as analytical as the conscious mind, which makes it open to limitless possibilities. It is here that you go to re-program your thoughts and actions, in order to create your reality.

Conscious Mind

Like that tip of the iceberg, this part of your mind is the one you are the most aware of, and it is the part of you that is the most limiting. Anything that you are immediately aware of, such as the sounds you hear, what and how well you see, and even your ability to pick out smells, are all examples of the conscious mind in action. Your immediate judgments about what is right and wrong, and your ability to analyze things, all comes from the conscious mind. However, it is through this process of judging and analyzing that the conscious mind also restricts us as it decides what is possible, and what is not. The conscious mind is that part that takes time to mull things over, think things through, and questions if you should or shouldn't do something. This thinking process can happen in a few seconds, but you are aware of the process. Too often if not checked, it will operate out of fear and ego, as these two elements are what will limit your thinking. Through meditation and hypnosis, you can learn to shut down the conscious mind for at least a short time in order to bring more clarity to a situation.

Where Does Ego Come in?

On this journey of self discovery and re-programming of your thoughts, you will undoubtedly come to odds with your ego. The ego likes to dwell in your conscious mind, where it can create all kinds of scenarios, and hand out advise on what is right or wrong. Even the pros and cons of situations can at times seem almost rational. It can be the ounce of self-confidence that pushes you to step out of your comfort zone, but unfortunately, it has a very bad habit of going too far. Like an emotional pendulum, the ego will swing from self doubt to a feeling of being better than everyone, from encouraging you to run everyone's life, to putting a great shield around you so you won't get hurt. It is the force that will stop you from apologizing, or encourage you to become judgmental. Most damaging is its ability to prevent you from recognizing your own contribution to your life's situations. The ego is the champion at blaming everyone else for your present circumstance. It is that nasty voice that convinces you that *"if only"* or *"once this happens"* occurs, then things will be okay. However, all too often, this is only ego's way of stopping you from realizing the wonderful potentiality that resides within you.

Ego is the king of all your fears, and will do everything to remind you of this. However, without the ego, where would your challenges be in overcoming obstacles along your life's path? You do require a boost of self-esteem and confidence to get you going on your mission. In order to help others, you want to feel worthy of carrying out a task, being knowledgeable and understanding. It is only at those times when you allow ego to be the supreme ruler that you will begin working out of the fear of losing control, fear of what others think, fear of not being good enough.Once you work from fear instead of your passion, the dreams fade away.

Learning to distinguish the voice of your ego, and that of your inner knowing or Higher Self, can be challenging at first. Always remember that you are here to learn, to experience life, and to create what it is you desire. There will often be experiences that do prevent you, at that particular moment in time, from reaching your goals, but more often it is your own thinking that is holding you back. The loud and impatient voice of ego shouting negative thoughts can block your inner creator from shining through. Taming this beast is a lifetime occupation, but once you come to recognize your own ego, and what fear drives it, you are well on your way to making things happen in your life.

The Choice to Fight, Flight, or Faint

In any given situation, you have choices on how to act or react. It may not seem so at the time, but you do. Even if you are physically unable to run away, to stand and fight, or to allow yourself to fall unconscious within your mind, you are making this decision. In your thoughts this all happens within a millisecond!

In your subconscious mind, you have numerous actions and reactions already stored, just waiting to go into motion once a trigger is activated. Let's use the example of a snake crossing your path, while you are out for a walk. Depending on what previous memory you have tucked away in your subconscious data base, will determine your reaction. When your conscious mind sees the snake, this message is automatically relayed to your subconscious mind, where it quickly ruffles through past experiences, not weighing out the positive or negative, but simply bringing forth a past response. Should you be like many people, and your past response has been to scream and run away, that is what your first impulse will be to do—you will choose flight. Perhaps you are more aggressive, and feel in danger. Before you know it you are throwing rocks at it, or grabbing sticks to force it out of your way—you fight. In extreme cases you may be one who cannot deal with the situation at all. Rather than making the decision of fight or flight, you choose to faint! Your past thoughts have created your present reality, and how you react to a given situation. Not all people react the same way, because everyone has their own thoughts, their own data base, and have made their own decisions on how to experience the present moment.

You can take the scenario with the snake, and replace the snake with any other situation that faces you. Take your present situation for example…your inner desire to make changes in your life. Is your ego bringing up past experiences, using them to create scenarios of failure? Do these thoughts influence you to make excuses why you cannot do something? Do you allow these thoughts to sway you away from accepting the opportunities when they arise, or in other words move in to flight action? Can you feel your pride taking over so that you base your decisions on what others think, rather than on what your heart desires, choosing to accept that things cannot change…stay, and fight? Or are you one who knows you need to change, but don't want to put the effort into doing so? Or would you choose to deny your part in that change so you close your eyes to what is really going on in your life—you faint?

Over the years all your life experiences, your thoughts and the words and actions of others have been stored away in your subconscious mind waiting for the right triggers to bring them out. If, as mentioned previously, these past thoughts make up 95% of your present thinking, don't you believe it is time to do some housekeeping, and clear out what no longer serves you?

Shaping Your Thoughts

So many people do not take the time to examine their own ideas and thought patterns to see if there is something they can do to make changes in their lives. Perhaps until today, you too had very little awareness of what you were thinking, or more importantly where those thoughts came from in the first place. Isn't it wonderful to know that you are now on your way to find the motivation, and methods to manifest what you desire into your life? You already know about your conscious and subconscious mind, and how your ego works. The next step is to begin the re-programming process.

What you decided to wear today, eat for breakfast, and even if you were going to be happy or sad, all started first in your mind with a simple thought. Look around you. Everything that you use in your daily life was first a thought in someone's mind; the furniture you sit on, the house you live in, the car you drive, were not always there. The idea was what put the creative thought process into action. It also took that someone overcoming the ego telling him/her that they couldn't do something, being strong enough to think outside the box, and let go of the fear of failure and objections of others. These people knew that their ideas were achievable somehow, and in some way at the right time.

So what makes this type of person any different than you? *Nothing*! Well, maybe one small thing; you may be limiting yourself by the walls you have built around you in the past. Beginning today, you can break down those barriers, and build your own dreams, ideas, and aspirations. You are the only one who truly knows what is going around and around in your mind. It is absolutely and entirely up to you to allow this process to begin. Once you accept this challenge, there is no stopping you in achieving what you desire.

If you are not taking time to ask yourself what it is you want and why, you are no doubt following the life plan others have for you, want to live through you, your whole life was not your own. Then what? *Change it*! Until you make your mind up to change, you will find yourself sitting in the same place this time next year. Think about it for a moment. Thoughts create your reality, how you feel, how you look at the world, and the chances you are willing to take, all begin first in how you think. If in your mind's eye you are already creating negative outcomes, excuses, and scenarios, then how can you expect to make positive change?

Are Your Thoughts Controlled?

One of the biggest trips the ego takes is the one of control, power, and manipulation of others. When you look around the world, it is easy to see where wars have been fought, laws have been made, and dogma put in place. Relationships based on one person's ideals may be used to control the lives of others, so that someone gets to call the shots for everyone, and the ego feels like god. People will allow this abuse of power out of fear of the repercussions that may follow. However, it is only when they realize that no matter what is done to them, no one can get into their minds and make them think any certain way. When they understand that they are reacting to the controller out of fear, and not out of their own thinking of what is right to do, they then gain the strength to put their thoughts into positive action. The controller governs by fear of losing control, and not out of love and compassion. As long as the controller fears, negative solutions will always be their method of rule.

Every life event you have will be experienced uniquely by you, and the others involved. Take something as simple as going to a party. You go with the expectation of having a great time, and have been thinking about the people you will meet, and the fun you will have, and you can actually feel it before you even get there. In your mind you have decided it is going to be a great evening no matter what. Now, you have a friend going along with you, who maybe has not had that great a day, and all she can think about is the argument she had before leaving the house. Right now her thoughts are on feeling upset—an emotion she has decided to hold onto into the evening. You both arrive at the same party, are greeted by the same jovial host, you can hear the same music, see the same people, and eat the same food. However, you have come into this energy knowing you are going to have a great time, whereas your friend decided long before she got there, she was not going to enjoy herself. Unless she is willing to change her thoughts about her own ability to share in the excitement and happiness that surrounds her, no matter what you say or do will convince her she is having anything, but a horrible time. The same would go for you. Her negative feelings can begin to attach to your energy, even beginning to make you feel drained. You do have the ability to stop those emotions, and continue to have a good time. It will all depend on how each of you registers consciously your environment, what triggers are set off from your subconscious, and how much you listen to your ego. Wow! Going out can get complicated. Right? Remember, you are only influenced by others if you let them get into your head.

Hypnosis – Helpful, or Fanciful

If you are like a lot of people, you may not have a great deal of experience with hypnosis, other than what you may have seen on the movie screen or in night clubs. The fact is, your mind goes into hypnosis mode quite often, and you don't even realize it. Have you been driving along a familiar route, and all of a sudden wonder how you got to this intersection so quickly? Perhaps you can't remember passing the last street? Scary isn't it? Or you start out going along the same route you always take to go to work, but today you want to take a side street to run a different errand. However, before you realize it you have missed your exit, and are pulling into the work parking lot. How did you do that?

You most likely got lost in one of your 80,000 thought processes and drifted off somewhere in your mind's eye. Your conscious mind, which is suppose to pay attention to your body's activities, kept on working, but your awareness was somewhere else. Fortunately your subconscious mind remembers how to drive, and kept on guiding you along the familiar path, placing you in auto pilot. The conscious mind was the part of you that was to make the judgment call on any changes along the road. The subconscious mind was triggered by you starting out the same way, and was able to bring up a past experience therefore creating the reaction to your journey.

Hypnosis, when guided by a trained hypnotist, or through the use of self-hypnosis techniques, can assist you in uncovering the memories stored in your subconscious mind. Once there, you are able to make decisions on what no longer serves you, allow forgiveness and acceptance of yourself and others to take place, and to establish positive affirmations in this data base for future reference. Now when you think those 80,000 thoughts a day, at least part of your 95% of repeated thought patterns will included the revised and improved ideas you placed there during your hypnosis. Sometimes this happens immediately, and other times you will find you have to do some real work to amend or delete the old ways of thinking as they have a tendency to creep back in every now and then. The difference now is that you realize you have the ability to accept them as your present day truth, or to decide they no longer serve you, and send them to the recycle bin. The use of hypnosis can speed up this process for you if you decide this is a tool that will serve you. If you are in fear of being controlled by the hypnotist, perhaps you should do more research on the topic, or learn the self help methods. For either to be successful, remember you are the one in control of your thoughts. Ultimately, it will be your own decision to follow through with the affirmations, or let your ego break them down.

Have you ever considered how quickly you are to accept praise for all the great things you have accomplished, and to blame others when things go wrong? How often do the words: *if only, but, if it hadn't have been for, he/she made me feel,* creep into your vocabulary? In reality, you have the ability to choose your reaction to any situation, even if at the time it doesn't seem that way. How you experience the situation, the words spoken, the actions taken, and ultimately your interpretations of the event, are all uniquely your own. Just like in the previous example of going to a party with a friend, you could describe how you observe how she was experiencing the party, but that is all it is, an observation. The same if she was to attempt to describe your experience. No one else controls them, or completely understands them like you do. You may be influenced by someone else, and you influence others, but in the end, your personal emotions and thought processes are yours alone.

Empowered Through Thoughts

It may take some time, but once you come to understand and believe that your thoughts are you own, you begin to feel empowered. It brings the awareness that through your own thoughts, you can now start to create your own reality. Of course, it does take some work! There are times when you will no doubt be tempted to follow the masses, rather than taking the time out to discover how you feel, what your truth is, or where you want your life to lead you. Be influenced by the success of others, but remember that it's their path, and you can follow their example, but still create your own way of doing things.

Actually, it is by diving into the sea of universal consciousness, a place of all thoughts and actions, where you may receive insight, opportunities and, encouragement. The stories of another person's struggles and accomplishments can bring hope and inspiration by reminding you that you too have these same possibilities, just waiting to be opened up, and developed into your own manifestations. Use their life experiences, not in a way that mimics them, but rather in a new and improved way that is a reflection of your own uniqueness.

Turn those thoughts and spoken words into ones of *"I know I can do it"* not *"what makes me think I can do it", "they succeeded, so can I"* not *"they did that, but I am not like them".* Only you have the power and the ability to bring about the positive changes in your life, because after all, no one else knows what it is you truly desire. Sometimes you may even feel that you need a change, but cannot quite figure out what that change needs to be, so how do you expect others to know what to do for you? Now is the time to lead your own life, create your own goals, and live your dreams. It is time to *make it happen*!

Changing Your Thoughts

You are never too old, too set in your ways, or not smart enough to change your way of thinking. Actually if you decide you are any of these things, you have already created those ideas about yourself in your subconscious mind. Perhaps you grew up in an environment or relationship where you were told things or actions were taken against you that created feelings of low self esteem, unworthiness, or of being unloved or unlovable. Maybe the changes you want to make frighten you as the success will depend on how willing you are to step out of a comfort zone. Believe it or not, all this is wonderful! Identifying those memories, ideals and experiences that trigger negative responses, is very important in re-programming your response to them. After all, if you want different results, you have to respond in new ways.

Often there are fears, old memories, and thought patterns that you will need to address in order to move forward. Facing your fears is like taking down an old garden wall in order to gain access to the other side. You will need to break down the fears by recognizing them for what they are, and then be willing to do the work to move them out of your way. This is where being nonjudgmental and objective to a situation can be very difficult, but necessary if you are to gain control over your own thoughts. By stepping back from the event, and observing it through the questions of *"How did this serve me? What positive lesson did I take away from this?"*, you will gain new insight into how to break a pattern that no longer serves you. You can let go of fears, and more importantly see how far you have come. With this newly acquired strength, you will find the self confidence to make those changes you want in your life.

Fear is the greatest brick in that wall that you will have to break down. You will likely find that the fears are the foundation of all your negative emotional attachments to the events or memories that have been holding you back from having all those endless possibilities in your life. Your desire to belong to a group, or to receive acceptance in your family, can cause you to do things in such a way that serves others, but will leave you feeling empty and unfulfilled. This can go on for years, even a person's lifetime, without you realizing what you are doing.

Love on the other hand, guides you to work for the higher good of yourself, and in turn for others. When you live your own life out of love, you find you are able to see joy in yourself, those people around you, and in life in general. You feel this way because you have shed the heavy burden of always trying to please everyone else, and being left feeling short-changed in your own happiness. Again, love will guide you to see that how you feel about yourself and the actions you take are you own doing, and love does not blame others for your situation. It will bring you up to understand that you have the power to be and do anything you desire.

Who Am I?

When was the last time you asked yourself, *"Who am I?"* Take a moment to do that now, and listen to how you answer that question. It is so very important what you place after, *"I am"*. It sets the base for all questions, rules all your actions, and provides reasons for why you behave and interact the way you do in all areas of life. Your thoughts create your reality, so if you answer that question with I am stupid, you will not feel intelligent regardless of your education. If you answer I am fat, you will see yourself as overweight no matter what you do as far as diet and exercise are concerned. If you answer I am a loser, you will never win, no matter how the world sees your successes. You and you alone are the one who decides who you are, and that in time is what the world will come to see as well.

How differently would you feel about yourself if you were to answer that same question, *"who am I?"* with an answer such as, *"I am infinite possibilities, or I am the creator of my reality, or I am worthy to receive and give love and joy in my life."* By doing so, you take away the barriers that have been holding you back from making positive changes in your life, and tell yourself you can, will, and are worthy in doing so. At this moment in time perhaps you do feel unworthy, or you answer the question simply by answering with your name. That is okay, but you are encouraged to ask yourself this question often, and see how it changes, and how those changes are affecting your outlook on what you say and do.

If you are like most individuals walking the face of the earth, you are quick to find fault with some part of your physical body or habit you have, but when was the last time you told yourself that you loved who you are? More importantly, do you love yourself? Even mildly like who you are? You may have been brought up to feel it was selfish to think about yourself, love yourself, or even admit to liking who you are. If you do not feel loveable, then that is the image you put out to the world. Your reality is shaped by your own thoughts.

When you don't feel good about yourself, it will not matter what anyone says or does, you will not feel loved. Unless you feel good about yourself, you will never feel completely fulfilled because your inner self will be longing to be loved by the most important person…you! Maybe you do need some fine tuning, minor or even major adjustments to how you deal with life, but this is doable. You are the only one who can make this happen.

By learning to face those fears and negative memories, you can learn from them, and create new patterns of letting go, and moving forward. After all, there is no going back and changing things, but you can recognize that you did what you thought was the best thing at that particular moment in time. It is over, learn from it, and step forward. To keep thinking and doing things the same way, only keeps you in the past. You become like that hamster in a wheel constantly running, and turning the wheel, but going nowhere, and changing nothing.

The same is true about worrying about the future. It has not arrived yet, but you can put what you imagine into reality through your thoughts. If you are worrying about all the *"ifs"*, and *"could bes"*, then that is the reality you are designing for yourself. You are creating stress, worry, and robbing yourself of the joy that you deserve today. This worry can block you from taking advantage of opportunities that are presented to you today because you are living in fear of what might happen. Replace that worry with all the possibilities of what is yet to come. See that image in your mind's eye, and feel it like it has already happened.

Living in the moment is taking each second of the day as a life experience. What blessing has it bestowed upon you? What part of your manifestation has it exposed for you? How has it served the higher good of your life, and others? You are here to experience life, and that means every single moment of it. It is through the tears that we appreciate the laughter, through sadness we come to know joy, through a broken heart we understand compassion. All the moments of your day become part of that 95% of repeated memories you will have running through your mind tomorrow, and the next day. Hold onto the moments that serve you well, and be strong enough to let the others ones go.

All this takes patience and practice. Being more mindful of your thoughts and actions is not something you do, but rather something you become. Soon you will realize you are more in touch emotionally, physically, and spiritually, with how your body and mind feel and operate. You become in touch with how one affects the wellness of the other. Through a daily practice of taking a few moments of silence where you bring awareness to your mind, body, and spirit, you will soon discover how your thoughts, not only manifest material things in your life, but your over all well-being. By feeling the connection within, and to the world and universe around you, will pull more of the same positive energy in to your life.

One of the biggest hurdles to overcome can be the temptation to be judgmental of, not only others, but of yourself. It is often the harsh judgment you have placed upon your past deeds that fills you with regrets, remorse, anger, and even self pity. It can be from this dark place of judgment that all the criticism, self-doubt, and even dislike, can feed the ego, and in return hold you back from believing you are even worthy of having what you desire. Sound familiar?

Becoming objective and observing a situation will take some practice, but it is essential if you want to learn from your past so you can be joyful in your present, and manifest your future. What if you looked back with the attitude that you did the best you could at a moment in time in your life? Yes, it is easy to see if something that you feel now was the right thing or not, but at that moment, your feelings were different, your vibration was different, and your emotions were different than they are at this moment, while looking back. Sometimes it is hard to be honest with yourself, and admit that perhaps you were not working from a place that was for the higher good. Okay, now move forward, because you cannot go back.

When you are regressing, become aware of not only how you feel emotionally, but how your physical body is feeling. Can you understand now how what you are thinking can affect your over all well-being? EVERYTHING begins with your thoughts, and how you react, act, and feel. This is why it is so important that you realize how amazing you really are, and powerful in creating your own reality. If you have difficulty at this moment deciding what it is you wish to have in your life, can you imagine what it is you want to feel? After all, at the end of the day it is all about how something, or someone, or an experience, made us feel. That is what our bodies and spirit relate to and respond to.

Creating a Positive Affirmation/ Auto-Suggestion

Before you begin using self-hypnosis or meditation to enter your subconscious mind, it is necessary to first create a positive affirmation, also known as an auto-suggestion that relates to what it is you wish to manifest in your life, or motivation to start the manifesting process. Again, remember it is your own thoughts that shape your reality, so choosing the best words is important. Using only positive words in your affirmation, you will instill a positive outcome. By writing it down, you are making an even more powerful contract between yourself, your Higher Self (spirit), and the Universe, to step in and help you out. Take this process a little further by speaking the affirmation out loud, and it makes it even stronger. It is like you are telling yourself what you are thinking, what you wrote out is true to you, and that is because it is! Your thoughts shaping your destiny—how wonderful is that?

How do you Perceive Yourself?

First, take a look at how you view yourself. After all, if you are attempting to make changes in your life, to gain more self control and empowerment over your own destiny, it is important to understand how you see yourself.

Are you ready to start looking within, and sorting out your own thoughts? Here is a list of descriptive words to help you get started. Do you consider yourself to be:

Beautiful	Ugly
Smart	Stupid
Handsome	Plain
Inferior to others	Superior to most
Competent	Incompetent
Outgoing	Introverted
Brave	Cowardly
Open	Closed
Emotional	Unfeeling

Do you feel somewhere in between? Or do you feel one way sometimes, and other times another way?

Step One: Take the next ten minutes to think about your characteristics. Write down the words that you feel best describe you. You can use the words from the above list, or add your own words. Be honest.

Step Two: Now go back over the list you have just created, and after each word, say to yourself, *"I perceive myself as ____________ and this is a choice I have made."*

How did that make you feel when you heard yourself say these things out loud? Did you have some negative feedback?

Step Three: Look at your list again, only this time decide if you want to continue looking at yourself that way, or is now the time to literally see yourself in a new light, a more positive and inspiring way. If you are ready to change, circle the word. This time, speak each circled word, one at a time, and as you do, say to yourself, *"I can choose to continue seeing myself as ____________, or I can choose to focus on my natural strengths and abilities instead."*

How did this make you feel? Did you feel more in control?

You need to look at the words that are presently making up your vocabulary, and even omit many of them. Our minds are very interesting devices that record and save information in a certain pattern. For example, you say to yourself *"I cannot eat sugar and fats."* Now, this could be a true enough fact, but the mind doesn't register the negative word cannot, but rather records eat sugar and fat. What happens next? You are now craving sugar and fat because your awareness goes to where your thoughts are, and in this case the thoughts are on sugar and fat. If this was something you wanted to overcome, you would have to create a more positive suggestion, *"I will make healthy food choices."* In this way you are replacing your previous desire of eating sugar and fat with your desire. To make it even more powerful, replace *"I will"* with *"I am"*, and in that way you are speaking in the present moment, not an intention for the future.

The suggestions are positive, and as though you are already doing them. You imagine in your mind's eye what is your desire, and see it as if it were already in your life…believe it can happen, and be open to receive the opportunities as they arise to make it happen.

By focusing on what you cannot do, or thinking negative thoughts about yourself, creates a picture of yourself that is extremely narrow, lacking in potentiality, and limiting. Focus instead on your strengths, and use them to become all you can be. This is the way to manifest what you want in your life.

Words to look out for!

The following two words are ones everyone seems to fill their vocabulary with from sunrise to sunset. How often do you use these words, even when your intentions are positive, and meant to be inspiring to yourself and others? Becoming aware of the meaning and frequency of the words you use every day will help you to uncover just how much they have shaped your present world. By changing them, you can then create a better reality.

Try – it implies that you will not succeed. When you say you will *try* to do something, meet someone, or be somewhere, in your mind, you already have doubts that what you are speaking of will actually happen. Be honest, have you ever been invited somewhere, and you really didn't want to go but instead of saying no you answered, *"I will try and make it"* knowing you had no intention of going, but would rather welcome anything that would prevent you from keeping the engagement? By saying the word *try*, you put the intention or desire out to the Universe to find a way to stop you from following through, or to at least make for a difficult time making things come together so you could go.

Want – is to say you would like it, but it is unattainable. In other words you feel you are in the position of want, or a place of being unworthy to receive, or what you desire is so high above you that it can never happen. When you use the word want, it is a half-hearted desire, or a lazy request, because you state what you would like on one hand, but just as quickly feel you do not deserve the opportunity or have the power to see it through.

Any words that indicate you are a victim, hands over the control to another person or situation. Here are a few examples:

Abused	Abandoned
Controlled	Cheated
Duped	Exploited
Intimidated	Manipulated
Rejected	Deceived
Suckered	Betrayed
Neglected	Humiliated

There are people and situations who certainly have said or done things in your life that triggers these feelings in you. This occurs when you allow yourself to replay these events over and over again to yourself, in thoughts such as I am cheated, I am betrayed, I am deceived. These words describe another's actions, not your feelings, and in using them to describe how you feel, you are actually handing control over to them. Your goal now is to declare emotional freedom from the victim stance. Remember, what you place after *I Am* are the most powerful words you can say to yourself.

Look at the following examples to help you see what the connection between these actions, and the feelings they create:

Action	**Feeling**
Betrayed	Naïve
Cheated	Foolish
Exploited	Empty
Manipulated	Defenseless
Neglected	Invisible
Abused	Powerless

Creating Your Personal Auto-Suggestion

Only you truly know what it is you desire and need at this moment in time. Now is the time to create your own auto-suggestion that you can use to encourage yourself on the path of self empowerment. It doesn't have to be a long winded speech, but it does need to resonate with what you long for at this present moment. Keeping in mind that the suggestion needs to be *positive* only, as your subconscious mind does not sort things out for you, but rather stores them for you to draw from. These suggestions can be used during your self-hypnosis time, repeated throughout the day, carried with you in your pocket or purse, or repeated before going into meditation so that you can feel them, and be reminded of their words.

Here are some examples of a positive affirmation. You can create a one sentence affirmation or a short paragraph, but remember to keep it positive and to the point of what it is you are manifesting.

I feel good about my commitment to seek inner peace and balance.
I deserve the time and effort it takes to bring my mind, body and spirit into complete harmony.
I have the power within myself to let go of any regrets, remorse or guilt I may be holding from the past, and let go of any worries about the future. Holding onto these negative emotions only robs any joy today.
I am in control...I have the choice between grievances or miracles, and today I choose the miracles.
I am willing to make the necessary adjustments in my life to make things happen.
I am worthy of love, and I am open to receive and give love.
I am finding joy in my life, work, and relationships.
I am a beautiful being of light with the ability to create my own reality.

Using Self-Hypnosis to Change Your Thinking

Many people become afraid when the word "Hypnosis" is used. Remember, hypnosis is the process of accessing your subconscious mind so you can clean house on all that stored data in your brain closet. Whether you are simply adding a positive affirmation to bring about changc, to manifcst somcthing, or to amcnd, rc-arrangc, or discard old thought patterns and triggers, the steps are the same. Once you learn these tools, you can incorporate them in a daily meditation practice to help you to go deeper into your meditation, and to continue to bring what you need into your life. You don't need fancy equipment, drugs, or a special location. You only need your desire and willingness to be in the driver's seat of your own destiny. How wonderful is it to know you have the ability to make it happen?

Follow these simple steps and you will find yourself creating your own reality:

- Find a comfortable space where you can sit quietly for just a few minutes, undisturbed by people, pets, TV, phones or computer. It will be only you, and your affirmation.
- First you will be doing deep breathing - your body's built in relaxation tool. By focusing on your breath, you are able to release stress, and bring your awareness to your intention. It helps to close your eyes so you can shut out all other distractions around you. Now, take in a long slow deep breath through your nose. Hold for the count of two, then slowly release the breath through your mouth.
- Repeat the deep breathing for about three to five times, and feel your body begin to relax.
- Then you will repeat your positive affirmation that you have created prior to doing this self-hypnosis. Repeat it at least three times. At first you may have to read it, but soon you should be able to say it to yourself, while sitting quietly with your eyes closed.
- Begin taking slow, deep breaths again to bring your awareness back to your physical body, and to your space.
- Open your eyes, feeling relaxed and inspired!

Congratulations! You have now taken the first step in being empowered to bring change into your life! Repeat this process every day. Be patient with yourself as it has no doubt taken years of programming and life experiences to put your present thoughts into your mind. It will take a little bit of time to reprogram yourself. Write out your affirmation, and carry it with you so you can read it and say it throughout the day, especially in those moments when you feel fears and doubt sneaking into your thoughts. You have conceived the idea, now it is time to believe you can MAKE IT HAPPEN!

Chapter Two:

What Moves You?

"When you do things from your soul, a river moves through you. Freshness and a deep joy are the signs."~ Rumi

One of the most important discoveries you can make about yourself is what moves you, or in other words, what is it that motivates you? Do you find you are basing your actions and reactions on what others will say, think, or do, rather than on what you feel would be right at that moment in time? Do you ever even stop to think about whether you are acting out of fear or love in any situation? Are your words true to you, or are you an echo of someone else's beliefs and reasoning?

From the time of your birth, you would have observed with innocent eyes, the actions of all those people around you. Your own parents, guardians, teachers, and members of your community, would instill in you their culture, faith, and ways of thinking. Not yet knowing your own truths, you accepted what you were shown, and told to be the only way things could be done, what you were capable of, or how the world works. Unless at some point in your life you begin to expand your thinking, and begin asking questions, the ways of others are adopted, and accepted by you as your own thoughts. When the things you are taught or take in from the world around you are positive and encouraging, then you will no doubt have been inspired to become all you can be. However, should your environment have been less than desirable, negative, and controlled, you may find it virtually impossible to see yourself outside of, or more evolved than, those around you, especially in this situation, understanding that you can make changes in your life by changing your thoughts. This will be the fuel you need to spark the flame within and find the motivation you need to get the fire of hope, desire and manifestation roaring. Clearing out the thoughts that no longer serve you, and replacing them with positive motivational ideals is key to living in love, rather than fear.

When you allow yourself to create out of love, rather than fear, your whole being will be filled with excitement and anticipation of what is yet to come, instead of the fear of making a mistake, what others think, or failure. You feel joy in every moment, with a willingness to try new things by stepping out of the comfort zone you have previously built around yourself. Often this comfort zone turns into a jail, keeping you from seeking your path, and limiting you in all areas of your life. Living out of love grants you the security in knowing that all is as it should be in this moment in time. Even those times when you fall miserably, you have the confidence to pick yourself up, dust yourself off, and go at it again, only this time in a new and improved way. There are no mistakes, only experiences, and you now know your purpose is to learn from these life lessons.

Living out of fear creates ties that emotionally, spiritually, and often physically, bind you in a situation, relationship, belief system, and un-nurturing environment. Should these fears be ones that were instilled into your subconscious as a child, you may not even realize you are living out of fear. Getting to the root of what moves you is important, especially when you need to change your outlook. You are the only one holding yourself back, and it is now time to step out of your own way.

Success at manifesting your goals is based on your personal feeling of accomplishment, not on the judgment of others. In North America we tend to determine if someone is successful by how much money they make, what job title they hold, or their popularity with the news media, but are these really bench marks we should be using? Should we be judging at all? Remember, we are all on our personal life journey, and in the end it will be what we have learned, and the feeling we leave behind that people will remember. You may think having more money, a bigger house, or fancier clothes, will make your life complete, and then you will be happy. However, if you are basing your entire happiness on *"things"*, and what other people think—something you have no control over—you will always be short of reaching your goals.

Buddha defines success in this way, *"Success is not the key to happiness. Happiness is the key to success. If you love what you are doing, you will be successful."*

What is Joy?

Every moment of your life, you have the opportunity to experience, either an emotion that brings you pleasure, pain, happiness, sorrow, love, or fear. In just a few short milliseconds, your conscious mind takes in what is going on around you, which triggers a reaction from your data file in your subconscious mind, and you react—laughing, crying, fleeing, fighting, or frozen on the spot—all based on your inner stored records from past experiences.

When setting your new goals, take time to go deeper into your own emotions, and find what it is that truly makes, or would make you happy. If happiness brings success, then this should be the first thing to uncover, and either bring it back into your life, or start it growing in order for success to follow. Is happiness enough, or is there something that goes even deeper into your being? What if you were to find pure, unadulterated joy? Wouldn't that be even a greater gift to you? The words happiness and joy are often used interchangeably, but there really is a great difference between them. Happiness is something that you can feel in a moment, and it can be gone just as quickly. It brings a smile to your face, a warm fuzzy feeling to your heart, and kind words to your lips. Joy, on the other hand is a constant. It goes deep into your heart centre, and takes up residence there. You can still experience the negative emotions, but through it all you have an inner knowing that joy is guiding you, comforting you, and being expressed in your actions. When you allow your life to be joyful, you look at the world through positivity, love, compassion, and a determination to bring that joy into everyday life.

This joy is your passion, what makes you smile, your uniqueness, and ultimately what moves you. When you were a child, you were born with joy because you were straight from the source of pure love, and knew nothing else. Then as you grew, you experienced life on this planet with all its ups and downs, curves and hills, and often it is on this journey that you may have left behind the joy you felt as a child as you allowed the world around you to shape your thoughts and ideas. Our culture teaches us to play it safe, follow the program, adults don't play, age means slowing down and stop creating. WRONG! You are a beautiful being of light in a human body here on this little blue planet to live, become love, and to expand your horizons every moment of your life. You are entitled to joy in your life. Now is the time to reclaim that right you were born with, and once re-discovered, you will find the limits you previously placed around your life will soon fade away.

Finding Joy

"We are shaped by our thoughts; we become what we think. When the mind is pure, joy follows like a shadow that never leaves."~ Buddha

Take a few moments right now, and ask yourself, *"What brings me joy?"* Not just a short moment of happiness, but true joy. It is something that not only makes you smile on the outside, but you feel it on the inside as well. It can be something huge or small, involve just yourself, or a group of people, something silly or serious, but whatever it is, you are the one who feels uplifted by doing it. Perhaps you will have to think back to your childhood, and remember those moments of joy. If you are like many people, you have left behind those childhood games and activities because you think now that you are all grown up, you can't or shouldn't do them anymore. However, hidden in those memories is a special and precious gem of joy.

Now that you have your mind thinking about joyful things, take it a step further, and take the time to write down three things you could start doing right now, this moment in time, that would bring that joy back into your life. You may not be able to do these things exactly like you once did, but how can you incorporate those activities in your adult life? You may be surprised at how difficult this is to do at first, but stay with it. Do you find yourself making excuses why you cannot do them? Push that reasoning aside, pretending if you must, that you have absolutely no limitations.

All those excuses are fear based; usually what others will think and say, and the fear of failure. You should realize by now that you cannot please everyone, and by continuing to think that you should, and can, really sets you up for disappointment. This thinking steals your joy, or rather you give your joy away. After all, it is your choice to live out of love or fear. You may even use the excuse of being too old, too young, too poor, too big, too small, or just plain too afraid to step outside of your comfort zone, and be yourself.

Stop! Change the thought pattern into how you can, and let your imagination guide you. What if you were to ask yourself, *"Why not me?"* instead of *"Why me?"* or *"I could do that"* in place of, *"I can't do that."* It may not be easy at first, but if you allow yourself the gift of patience and time by taking one small step each day, you will be delightfully surprised to find joy easing its way back into your heart.

Making this change may also mean taking a good look at your environment. Are you surrounded by positive, encouraging people, or are they negative in their own lives, and how they speak to you? It is hard for a seed to take root if it is kept in the darkness, but give it sunlight and water, then it will grow. Like the seed, you may need to place yourself in the company of like-minded people, who bring light into your life and encouraging words to feed your growth. Be mindful of the company you keep, and the influence it is having on your thoughts and actions. It can be quite easy to slip into a pattern of doing what others say you should, or you feel they want you to do, in order to gain approval. What you are really doing is handing over your life to them, and living their life, not your own. You are not able to change how someone else thinks, acts, or lives their life, and the very same goes for you. Ultimately it comes back to you making the choice to make changes, create new ideas, and begin to manifest those things that better serve you today. In this way you are in control of having joy in your life, and not allowing someone else to decide if you deserve it, or letting them take it away from you.

Often when you are thinking about what you desire at this moment in time, it will be something tangible, like more money, a better job, a new car etcetera, and that is fine. However, it serves you well to go even deeper in your desires to find out why you are looking for these things? For example: if you are like many people, maybe you would like more money because you feel then you could buy the things you really want. Okay, fair enough. Now, why would you want those things? Is it because you feel they would make your life easier? Make you *"look"* better in front of others? Will it bring you happiness, and/or success? Maybe what you are really looking for is a sense of security, joy in your life, or inner peace that you feel would come if you were not worrying about money. Funny thing with money though, the rich and poor have the same issue…they never feel they have enough, and worry about getting more of it, or losing it! The sense of security in this case may never be met until you rediscover what brings you joy, not just the momentary happiness that all those things bring you, but the knowing that no matter what happens, you trust the Universe will take care of you, and you can create a new beginning.

Once you have decided on what it is you desire, and why you desire it, take a moment to examine it even a bit closer. Are you making your decision out of love or fear? If it is out of fear, you are either shaping your future based on what others will think in order to impress them, change them, or you are getting even with someone. Ego is the pilot in this seat as it drives fears, judgment, and negative thinking. On the other hand, your *Higher Self* will always work for the higher good, or what is best for you and others. It welcomes joy, positive energy, and experiences into your life. Since joy is anchored in pure love, anything you desire that has its roots in joy is coming from love, not fear. Once joy begins to flow in and through you, be prepared for opportunities to be opened to you in a variety of ways.

Even though you may think you know the best way for you to achieve your goals, often the Universe will provide a totally different way for you to travel. Seemingly innocent conversations can lead you to meet the right people, be in the perfect place at the right time, or hear about an opportunity you have been waiting for. Even those moments that at first appear to be stalling you, or stopping you from moving ahead, can be resting points for you so you can regroup, and evaluate your journey. Once you trust your instincts and allow yourself to be open to all possibilities without judgment or fear, you will be truly amazed at what you can create.

Becoming Joy

Now that you know what brings you joy, what you desire, and how to unite these two, you will want to imprint this thought into your subconscious mind. This way you make it part of your data file so that it is part of your 95% repeated thoughts of your 60,000 to 80,000 daily thoughts. Here is a short exercise using visualization to help your do just that:

- Once you make yourself comfortable in a place free from distractions, close your eyes.
- Without judgment, and with the belief that all things are possible, see yourself achieving your goal. What will you look like? See it now.
- Now for the really important part, you allow yourself to feel what it will be like to get what you desire. What positive feeling is reinforced?
- Allow this feeling to flow through your body, mind, and spirit, as though it has already happened. You may even feel a smile come across your face. Let it happen!
- As you sit visualizing this success, feel the joy go deep into your soul. Allow this joy to be your motivation.
- At this point, you may wish to repeat the positive affirmation you created earlier for this manifestation. By using both together, you instill even deeper, your intent to create your own reality.
- When you are ready, inhale deeply, then as you slowly exhale, open your eyes.

Repeat this exercise daily. The most effective times are first thing upon rising in the morning, and just as you are going to bed at night. This way you start your day with a positive affirmation and thought shaping image, and by ending your day with the same affirmation and visualization, you will be sure to imprint this image into your subconscious mind as well as letting the Universe know you are open to its help.

What if You Can't Feel Joy?

One of the hardest lessons, but the most important one to learn through this process, is that it will not always be super easy. If you remain true to yourself and your desire, you will overcome any obstacle. Patience and practice are the two main ingredients in this recipe for success. The next one is to trust that everything happens when the time is right. When you start putting your trust in, not only your own ability to manifest, but in the hands of the Universe, it can get a bit scary at times. After all, you are trusting in something you cannot see. It is faith that the intention you put out into the world will find its way back to you, only ten, or even a hundred times greater.

You may be tempted to give up and go back to your old way of being, and slip back into your comfort zone. It is so easy to get distracted by the daily grind of going to work, family, physical illness, and all else that life can throw at you. Remember that it is through the trials and tribulations that you will discover your own life's lessons. It is during those times of overwhelming sadness that you will learn to appreciate happiness, through the tears of sorrow. You will realize love, and by facing your fears, you will come to recognize your own inner strength. Maybe you have decided it will take too much effort to reach your goals, or you are having the battle of the century within between *Ego* and *Higher Self,* Sometimes Ego seems to be winning. Do not despair! This only means you are a spiritual being having a human experience.

Everything comes about for a reason. What lessons are you learning from this experience? What if this obstacle is not really something horrible holding you back so you cannot reach your goal, but rather a way of making you take time out to re-evaluate the direction you need to take? Perhaps it is the Universe's way of saying, *"slow down, re-group, check your road map, you have gotten off course, and we have a better plan for you!"*

You may even feel that you have completely lost your way and darkness has consumed you. During these times the light, or any form of positive energy, never mind your joy, may be impossible to see, feel, or touch, in your present moment. As difficult as it may seem, you still can choose to live free of the darkness by reminding yourself that darkness does not really exist, but rather it is the measurement of the absence of light. That would suggest that light is always there, even in a very small amount, in order to be measured. By being aware of your thoughts, you may find yourself falling back into your patterns, blaming others for your situation, or using excuses for yourself and others to justify what is happening around you, and even how you are feeling. Constantly, you have the choice to decide what type of life you will have, how you will feel, and where you will go. It all begins and ends with your concept and belief in yourself, and your ability to manifest what you want in your life. Hold onto to your dream, and allow even a tiny spark of joy to light up your life, and soon you will be back on track.

Time to Get Moving

Are you choosing a life of abundance, or one of poverty? Are you striving to live in happiness, or in anger? Are you allowing love to flow through you and out into the world, or are you living in fear of being hurt and closing yourself off to all opportunities to receive love? Do you feel worthy to receive good things in life, or are you convinced your things will always fall through? You are the only one who controls these thoughts, and once you truly understand this and believe you have endless possibilities, the sooner you create what you desire. You and everything are made up of energy, and energy cannot be destroyed, but it can be transformed. The energy, or the positive or negative energy you put out into the Universe, is what will come back to you tenfold or more. Decide what you want to come into your life, then find ways to send that same energy into the world. In this way you are telling the Universe that you no longer fear receiving this positive returning energy into your life. For example if you are feeling lonely, and want this to change, go visit others who may be lonely, call someone, write a letter to someone, or even volunteer your time to help someone else. Many want more financial abundance to flow into their life. If you are not willing to give even a little of what you have to someone else, you are building a wall of fear of poverty, and in return more poverty is created in your life. By giving, you are breaking down this wall. It doesn't have to be money, but it can be a smile, a kind word, or a measure of your time. It is through the act of giving that you open yourself to receive the gifts others and the Universe will send to you. To bring joy into your life, you need to shed the negative emotions of anger, resentment, sadness, and the ego's destructive nature, and allow love and compassion to guide you.

There is no time like the present to get the wheels of change in motion. After all, since your thoughts create your reality, what you are thinking and believing as you read this are beginning to form your future. It is perfectly okay to take small steps to move forward, after all, depending on your situation, any change may feel huge for you at this moment in time. That actually is great! Remember, what you put out comes back with increased energy, so even what may seem like a very small movement can actually end up the greatest victory. Every step taken is one step further on your path to joy and success in fulfilling your desires.

Are you ready to take control of your own life, and make things happen? Well, what are you waiting for? Pull out your journal, piece of paper, computer page, and get to work!

- Think of one thing, no matter how small that would help you to begin your journey to bring what you desire into your life. What one thing, right now, can you change to help the flow of positive energy come into your life?
- Write this down: In this way you are creating a contract with yourself. It has been proven that those who not only think change, but set out their goals on paper, then say them out loud, are far more successful at reaching their goals than those who do not. Again, it is the intent that creates your

reality.

- Now it is time to visualize this change.
- Make yourself comfortable, take a few deep breaths, and close your eyes
- Repeat the affirmation you made earlier
- Visualize your desire as though it were already happening in your life
- See yourself eliminating any obstacles, self-doubt talk, and fears that may appear. To help with this, imagine you are holding a beautiful golden sword, and you can cut the cords that are attached between you and your fears, so that you are free to move forward with your desires.
- Every time you manage to cut a cord, or step closer to your desire, you have a feeling of accomplishment flow through you. You will feel motivated to move faster with renewed strength and determination.
- See and feel yourself taking that first step, and making it happen!

Chapter Three

What Do You Fear?

"Love is what we were born with. Fear is what we learned here."
~ Marianne Williamson

You know in your heart what you desire. You have written it down, and even done the exercise visualizing yourself successfully meeting your goals, but you don't feel as though anything is changing. It is during times such as this that you need to go a bit deeper into your own data base of past thoughts and beliefs to see what fear is holding you back.

At the base of all of your reasons, and seemingly justified excuses, there lies a fear of something or someone holding you back. Often these are ideas that have been instilled in your mind from birth, through a misfortune, or from your own lack of confidence in your personal ability to succeed. Fear can be helpful as an emotion to alert you to dangers as it heightens your senses, making you more aware of things around you. However, when these fears begin to guide and rule your judgments and decisions, they then create blockages, which in turn can stop you living your life to its full potential. Eventually, when you allow fear to guide you, it robs all joy from this moment in time, because all you experience is the fear. Remembering that what you think creates your reality, when you choose to live in fear, that is the life you are making for yourself.

Back in chapter one, you learned that 95% of your thoughts are actually repeated from past experiences and memories, whether they are from five minutes ago, or lifetimes ago. These ideas run over and over again in your mind. Unless you take the time to sort these out, let go of what no longer serves you, and release the ideas based in fear, you will begin creating a reality you may not wish to have. Sorting out what is real to you, and what is a fear that has expanded and become seemingly a reality, can be difficult at first, but oh, what a relief you will experience as you begin this process. You can always learn from these thoughts as they contain life lessons from past experiences, good and bad. It is in the sorting through and facing the fears that you will discover what is stopping you from moving forward, and find ways to defeat it.

Many times you carry fears from your childhood. These can be the result of something traumatic that happened to you, or something innocently said to you that left an impression and reaction in your subconscious mind. As an adult, you are able to look back more objectively through grownup eyes, and in that way begin the releasing process. Again, patience and persistence are key, as it often takes time to fully understand you. Things will be revealed when the time is right, and you will definitely have an *"ah ha"* moment.

The Fear and Negative Thought Connection

Every thought you have, the decision and action you take based on that thought is a choice you make out of either love or fear, and in return will create either negative or positive energy. Love embraces all things based on the betterment and the higher good of all, which in turn generates positive energy within and around you. Fear, on the other hand, churns your thoughts and emotions in so many directions, stirring up past grievances, regrets, anger, and sadness, so it can in no way produce anything but more negative energy. This negative energy stops you from feeling and being complete. Your intention is so focused on the fear, that you miss the loving positive energy when it is presented to you, and in turn more fear and negativity is created. When you find yourself feeling these negative emotions, it is time to ask yourself, *"What am I afraid of?"*, then keep asking it until you reach the source of your fear.

Many people—and you no doubt have tried this yourself—believe they can suppress the fear, tuck it away by forgetting about it, not talk about it, or in some way ignore the whole situation for the rest of your life. Well, this is not possible. Your subconscious mind will tuck those fears away for you, but when triggered, the subconscious memory will pop it out, no doubt when you least expect it, and there will sit your fear bigger than life. If you have not done any programming on how to react to the fear, your emotions and body will automatically react the same way you did in a previous situation. Too many times this manifests itself in disease either emotionally, physically, or mentally. You don't want that now do you?

The crazy thing about fears is that to others they may be totally illogical, but to you they are very real. You may even tell yourself that you shouldn't be afraid, but still you are. Don't be too hard on yourself. Your thoughts are your thoughts, so what is real to you is real to you. The important thing to remember is that you do have control over what you think, how you react, and what actions you will take. Your fears are not who you are, but a part of the lessons you are here to learn. It is through learning to manage, overcome, and use your fears to your advantage that you will grow and become empowered to make changes in your life. Here are just a few of the most common root fears. Almost everything you may be afraid of, or what is stopping you from becoming the amazing person you are meant to be, can be found here.

Fear of Failure

Over the last century, we have come to place so much emphasis on society's definition of success. It is usually decided on how much money you make, by the house and neighbourhood you live in, what job or business you have, and so on. It's mostly based on material gain, and has little to do with your own personal happiness. It also is wrapped up in the fear of what others will think, instead of what you feel to be your own path and truth. The one thing that is so much worse than failure is living with the regret of never having attempted to do what it was you wanted to do because, without trying, you will never know how well it could have gone.

Fear of Success

Why would anyone be afraid of success? Isn't that what you are looking for all along? With success there often comes more responsibility, making more decisions on your own future and, *oh no*, things may change! Even if you desire change in your life, you may find you are allowing the fear of success to stop you from being all you can be, and stepping outside of your comfort zone to expand your horizons. Maybe it seems like too much work to stay there, or more likely you do not feel you are worthy of success. The ego steps in and talks you out of reaching your goals by placing fear in place of love, discouraging you from even trying, and often posing the question, *"Who do you think you are to deserve this?"* This fear shines by allowing self-sabotage to ruin your chance of getting ahead with your dreams.

Fear of Being Alone

No one really wants to be entirely alone, but there is a huge difference between being alone, and feeling lonely. Nothing is more devastating than being in a relationship where you feel more alone when you are in your partner's company than when he/she is away. Perhaps you belong to a group, whether it is your family, religious organization or workplace where you don't feel you fit in, but you stay because you fear being alone would be worse. Guess what? It isn't worse at all. Taking the time to become your own best friend, love yourself, and do things for yourself, will fill the emptiness you have been feeling. By believing you can bring yourself happiness and love, and not placing that in the hands of others, you are able to release loneliness, and enjoy each moment. Soon, you will find you are connecting to others of like mind, who love and honour you for the wonderful person you truly are.

Fear of What Others Will Think

Now this is a biggie for sure! There are very few people who have not experienced this fear at one time or another. Often those who are the most flamboyant, loud, and demanding, are actually in fear of what others think, so a show is put on as a distraction. Are the clothes you wear, the way you cut your hair, the beliefs you have, or the way you choose to eat, all based on what you think others expect of you? This fear weaves it way into almost every other fear, but once you find its hiding place, you can face it and release it too. Letting go of the fear of what others think is different than not caring how you make someone feel, but rather you find strength in your own truth, and you are willing to follow your path regardless of what others say or do.

Fear of Losing Control

This fear too is often enveloped with other fears. Abusive relationships are prime examples of the fear of losing control. It is this fear that drives the abuser to say and act the way he/she does with others. Having the *"power"* to control people is easy to see throughout history. Perhaps you have a secret you don't want others to know—the fear of what other will think here again—so you make every attempt to control all aspects of your life, whether it is your relationships, children, work, or how things are arranged in your home. You have a need to be in control because you are afraid if you lose it, your world will surely fall apart. In reality what usually follows if this goes on for too long is your over all well-being is affected, relationships fail, jobs are dissolved, and eventually your children get their own lives. One thing is for certain in this world; what you focus on will happen, so if you focus on losing control, you most certainly will.

Fear of Speaking Your Truth

Although circumstances may be such that speaking what you believe is actually unsafe, most times you are able to find ways to bring your truth into your life. Again, this is usually coupled with another fear. First and foremost, you will need to learn what your truth is, not that of society, your family, or friends, but what is truth to you? Your first step is to discover what it is you want to manifest, and what you believe to be the action you need to take to make this happen. Then you are in a position to let go of the fear of not only speaking of this truth to others, but living it. This release will enable you to see your dreams come to life sooner than you could ever imagine. It is important to remember that speaking your truth is only half of the communication. Learning to listen is equally important. Talking too much about what you think is your truth, but not listening to others could be a sign that you are still afraid of what others will think, or it could be that you have not convinced yourself that this is your truth.

Facing Fear

Welcome to the little blue planet filled with life lessons, and emotional experiences. Not all will be pleasant, but what you learn from each one is up to you. All those things you fear can be managed, but it has to be by you. If you think you have them tucked away somewhere safe, or out of thought, you must know by now that is not so. It is impossible to not think about what you fear, because in order to not think of anything, you must first bring that thought forward so you can then tell yourself, *"Don't think about that!"* So what do you do?

Now is the time to look those fears straight in the eye, and ask, *"What are you teaching me about myself and others? How are you holding me back from being the awesome person I was born to be?"*

Depending on how deeply rooted your fear is, you may find it helpful to get someone to assist you in this process. It isn't always easy to define exactly what your root fear is as you may have many other fears to go through to find it. Letting go of your ego long enough for you to start peeling back the layers, is the important first step. You may find it hard to even admit you have a fear of anything, but once you are determined to make things happen in your life, you will find facing your fears is the only way to move forward.

So what does facing your fears mean? Well, in the following visualization, you are going to literally do just that. Imagine your fears standing before you so you can look them right in the face. You will treat them with a positive attitude filled with genuine love and gratitude, but also a firmness of letting them go by cutting the cords that bind you as these fears no longer serve your needs. Believe it or not, most all fears have had a purpose in your life. They could have shaped you into becoming stronger, going places you would never have gone, opened your eyes to compassion, even have shown you a shadow side of yourself that you now want to send on its way. These fears have served their purpose, and now it is time for them to move on so you can fill your life with your positive affirmations, visualize your new reality, and make the changes in your life you want, instead of focusing on what you do not want. You will be pleasantly surprised at how quickly this process works.

This visualization may need to be repeated a few times as some of those fears can be hidden deep within your being, and you may feel quite an attachment to them. This is especially true for the ones from early childhood, and those from a past lifetime as they may be difficult to identify at first. This is where a trained Hypnotherapist or Spiritual Coach could benefit your progress.

Letting Go Of Fears

As in the previous exercises, begin by making yourself comfortable where you will not be disturbed for at least 15 minutes.

- Make yourself comfortable then slowly close your eyes
- Take five deep, long and slow inhalations through the nose, then slowly through the mouth. Feel your body relax more, and more, with each breath.
- As you become more relaxed, be mindful that this time, this place, is your safe place where nothing can harm you.
- Repeat three times to yourself, *"I am relaxed, I am in control"*
- Now, imagine one at a time, your fears stepping up in front of you. It may look like someone, or something, or just a dark shadow, but do not be afraid. You are in control.
- Imagine you can look straight at it, and take a moment to identify this fear. Is it fear of what others might think? Fear of losing control? Fear of failure? What fear is holding you back at this moment in time?
- From your heart, give it thanks for being in your life, and for the lessons it has taught you.

- Now, visualize cutting the cord that attaches you to this fear.
- When you make the cut, tell the fear to be gone as it no longer serves you.
- Send the blessing *Namaste*. (this means the God in me, and recognizes and honours the God in you)
- Repeat bringing up the fears before you, showing gratitude, recognizing the lesson it taught you, cutting the cord, and sending it off with *Namaste* for each one.

Don't be surprised if you feel very emotional during this exercise as you are bringing forward things you may have tried to forget or ignore. Remember, throughout the exercise that you are in control, performing this exercise from your safe place.

Chapter Four

Mind, Body and Spirit...Bringing it all together

"Health is the greatest gift, contentment the greatest wealth, faithfulness the best relationship."~ Buddha

As if having a conscious and subconscious mind is not enough, you are made up of three bodies; the emotional body, physical body, and spiritual body, or more commonly referred to as mind, body, and spirit. Once you learn to become aware of each of them. you will find you are more readily able to get to the root of any unbalances in your life. By doing this, you are then able to be more focused and centred, as you are living with inner peace, and over all well-being. It is very important to have these bodies working together in order to manifest what you desire, otherwise you will feel scattered, lost, and often experience ill health. It is all about discovering yourself, and realizing the wonderful power you already have to live your purpose.

The emotional body makes up the mind portion of this trio. When dealing with your conscious and subconscious mind, you are dealing with this body. It is here you make the choices between seeing the world through love, or fear, allow yourself to act from compassion, or it is this body that determines negative or positive decisions. This is your human side or personality, which experiences all things on this earth, all the emotions whether they come from sadness or happiness, pleasure, or pain, the emotional body feels it all. Since you make decisions, and create your reality from your thoughts, it is very important to examine this body, and take a survey on just what is directing you at this moment in time. Are you holding back based in your past memories, and perhaps fears? Are you frozen in time out of worry about what might be in the future, or are you allowing yourself to experience this moment, and thus shaping what you wish to manifest? It all starts here in the emotional body.

The physical body is the body that makes you human. Even though it appears to be a solid matter, science has proven it is not. Trillions of cells move constantly, ever changing to give the illusion of something solid and real. You can see it, feel it, and move it, but it is only a part of who you really are. Think of your body as your temple that houses your emotional and spiritual bodies. It is a vessel through which you have chosen to travel your life experience. As a temple you need to honour it, show gratitude for it, and learn from it. When the emotional or spiritual body are not in balance, that is when disease will manifest itself in the physical body. Most viruses, immune system illness, high blood pressure, and even cancers and heart disease, are all triggered by something out of balance in the other bodies. In the same way when something is physically wrong with you, it will affect how you feel emotionally and spiritually as well. It becomes quite a circle! However, by knowing this, you are able to begin healing the body by creating the thoughts of healing in your mind and believing them. It has been proven that those people who have a more positive attitude heal much faster than those who do not. Which would you choose?

The spiritual body is the real deal; this is your Higher Self, or Spirit. This is the body that carries all the memories from past lifetimes, knowledge, and the wisdom you have obtained from the Universe. This spirit, the real you, has chosen to be in this physical body at this time to experience the human emotions, and yes, the ego too so you can spiritually grow, and be all you can be during this lifetime. Many people have forgotten about their spiritual body, and in doing so, find they are experiencing times of loneliness, feeling lost or scattered, as though drifting without a purpose. As you become more and more evolved, you will actually begin to understand, and realize you are in contact with your spiritual body through expanding your intuition and awareness. During those times when you are able to objectively sit back, and without judgment, see the why and how events in your life have brought you to where you are today. With that knowledge, you are able to confidently chart your future. It is through understanding this body that you will learn trust, patience, and unconditional love, for yourself and others.

So what do the three bodies have to do with manifesting in your life? It is very difficult to see what you desire if you are holding onto negative emotions from the past, worry of the future, or focusing on physical pain. You are endless possibilities and the only one or thing that is limiting you achieving what is for your higher good at this moment in time is you. Your thoughts can make or break your creating your reality. If you are focusing on the pain you are experiencing, whether it is a physical or emotional pain, then you will only magnify it even more. Where ever you place your awareness, energy goes there. If you are focusing on the pain or negative feelings, then that is where your energy goes and creates more of the same. Instead visualize seeing yourself healed, moving forward, and accept the pain as a stepping stone on this journey. Like the fears, acknowledge it, then release it, and put in its place the reality you desire. See it in your mind's eye, feel it in your body as though it has already happened, recognize the fears and/or ego that may come forward to block you, release and be open to receive. It does take some work on your part, but you can and will make it happen.

Many holistic practitioners work with an understanding of the mind, body, and spirit connection. In order to totally cure the physical, you will need to treat the root cause as well. The following is a chart listing some examples of physical illnesses that are triggered by emotional and spiritual imbalances. This is not intended for you to use as a replacement of medical help but it will serve you well to take notice of how your emotional state influences your overall health.

Accidents	Accidents are most often an expression of anger, frustration, and rebellion. These emotions often cloud your decision making which in turn will create the environment for accidents to occur.
Anorexia or Bulimia	Self-hate, denial of life nourishment, feeling not good enough, are all contributors to the emotional and mental state of eating disorders. Healing of past experiences is often helpful.
Arms	Your inability to embrace others physically as well as not being able to let go of old emotions can lead to pain in the arms and joints.

Arthritis	A pattern of criticism of self and others as well as perfectionism makes life difficult on yourself. These negative emotions are again held in the joints causing pain.
Asthma	Any emotions that cause you to feel smothered such as being in a relationship where you are not allowed your own time, or if you are that person who smothers someone with affection. You may carry a guilt complex, or inferiority complex, causing you to be always attempting to please others.
Back	When it is the upper back that is affected, it can be brought on by a need to be supported emotionally. It can also be from feeling you are carrying the weight of the world on your back. It could be time to let someone else carry the load. Middle back can be a result of feeling guilt either in the present, or holding onto guilt, remorse and regrets from your past. It is rooted in the fear of others finding out about this guilt. Lower back pain is usually a result of burnout from worrying about money, and your sense of security. This sense of security can be financial or in a relationship.
Breasts	Over-mothering, a person, place, thing or experience can result in diseases of the breasts. This is especially true if you are holding on to resentment connected to this "mothering" feeling.

Burns, Boils, Fevers, Swelling, sores	Anger is the prime emotion that can trigger theses ailments. This negative emotion festers inside until it has to manifest on the physical body.
Cancer	Deep resentment, distrust, self-pity, hopelessness, helplessness are a few of the emotions that can trigger cancer. Again, recognizing that your thoughts can control your reality can go a long way in preventing as well as healing the physical body of disease. Stress is one of the main contributors to all triggers in disease.
Colon	Constipation is the inability to let go, lack of trust of having enough, and even hoarding. It is based in the fear of not having enough. Diarrhea is fear of holding on to anything in fear you will be hurt especially in the areas of family, culture, and even religious beliefs.
Ears	Earaches can be the result of anger and the refusal to listen. Ringing in the ears may occur when you are trying to determine what another is saying is true to you or not. It is during these times you may find it is too hard to accept what is said, so you choose not to hear.

Feet	Do you need to make a move? Step out of your comfort zone? Trouble with the feet may appear when you are hesitating in moving forward in your life.
Fingers	Each finger has its own meaning. The Index finger represents issues concerning the ego, anger, and fear. When it is the Thumb, you are usually giving in to worry about the future or things you cannot change. The Middle finger can be associated with anger, especially when it is on the right hand of a man, or when it is on the left hand of a woman. For both it can represent an inability to let go. The Ring finger meridian goes to the heart centre, which is associated with our emotions. Pain can be triggered when a union is severed, followed by grief of this loss. Last but not least it the Little finger. Often family issues will manifest as problems with this finger. Are you presently pretending something and living in the fear of being discovered? This will lead to discomfort with the Little finger.

Genitals	What are your thoughts on femininity or masculinity issues? Do you reject sexuality? Think sex is dirty and women's bodies are unclean.? This can also be a time for you to come to terms with who you are sexually. Bladder infections can occur when you are pissed off at a person or situation either in the present moment or you are still holding in hurts from the past. Vaginitis can be triggered when you are romantically hurt by a partner. Prostrate problems can be rooted in a feeling of self worth or the lack there of and the fear of losing sexual prowess Impotence again can be triggered through the fear or spite against your mate, and the fear of not being sexually "good enough. Frigidity often comes from feelings of sexual guilt, self disgust resulting from negative and abusive experiences from your past. PMS: denial of female cycles or female worth.
Head	The main trigger here is how you see yourself in comparison with the world around you. As well the feeling as though there is something radically wrong with yourself, others, or even the world, can cause issues with the head.
Headaches	*See head.* As well, stress, worrying about the future, living in regrets and judgment of the past will only deprive you of seeing the good around you today.

Heart	Heart is love and blood is joy. Heart attacks are a denial and squeezing out of love and joy. Holding onto negative emotions will feed this denial. Stress is stored in the heart centre, which will in time affect not only the heart, but the lungs and blood circulation.
Knees	Inflexibility, unable to bend, is a sign that your pride, ego, stubbornness, fear of change, and self righteousness are ruling your thoughts. In other words, you refuse to bend on an issue or decision, even when doing so could bring you comfort. Time to kick the ego out of the way.
Legs	Fear or reluctance of moving forward, not wanting to move. Your desire to stay put is usually a fear of change or taking a chance at the unknown. Varicose veins can be a result of remaining in a place of hatred.
Lungs	The fear of taking in all that life has to offer and the fear of giving back can create issues of the lungs. Having a negative outlook on life can be smothering. Emphysema can be triggered by a denial of the goodness of life and a feeling of inferiority.
Migraines	Anger and perfectionism leads to frustration and when held in day after day will trigger migraines.

Neck	Flexibility issues as well as holding onto stresses of the world around you. Often you feel as though you have to be the one who does everything, and you may refuse to ask for help.
Overweight	Seeking protection from being hurt or abused so you attempt to lose yourself in your weight. Many who have had an abusive relationship either as an adult or child are left feeling insecure and unaware of their inner beauty.
Pain	Follow the pain to its location and see what the triggers are for that part of the body. Again, holding onto fears and a sense of unworthiness may make you feel as though you are deserving of this pain.
Sinus	Irritated by someone? Do you feel blocked from following your own intuition?
Skin	Threatened individuality, or feeling as though others have power over you. You may be over sensitive or thin-skinned, and walk around always feeling as though everyone is out to get you. Your sense of security can determine the health of your skin.
Stiffness	Where there is a stiff body, there is usually a stiff mind! The inflexibility of your body is a fear of taking a chance. By remaining firm and set to your way of thinking, there is only one way of doing things your body and mind remain stiff.

Stomach	Inability to digest ideas and experiences. Who or what can you or cannot stomach? If you have insecurities about how you face the world and others, you could find yourself with stomach problems. The fear of what others think can cause a lot of havoc with the digestive system.
Strokes	Negative thinking, stopping of joy, forcing change of direction are all triggers to strokes. These emotions also contribute to stress and left unattended will eventually manifest physically.
Swelling	Stagnated thinking, bottled up fears, feeling trapped can cause swelling not only in the joints but in muscles too.
Throat	When you live in fear of change, combined with the inability to speak your own truth throat issues are sure to follow. Again, anger can also be a trigger as can bottled up creativity. Laryngitis or sore through is often a result of being too angry to speak. Tonsillitis or thyroid can be in combination of stifled creativity. What is it that is true to you or your own creative path?
Tumors	Do you tend to dig up old hurts? Do you bring up a negative experience over and over again to the point that it cannot heal? Tumors can be triggered as a result and show up anywhere in the body.

Chapter Five

Meditation and You

"Half an hour's meditation each day is essential, except when you are busy. Then a full hour is needed." ~Saint Francis de Sales

Depending on where you live, who you ask, and what your particular belief system may or may not be, the definition of meditation may vary. Although the words prayer and meditation are often used interchangeably, there is a subtle difference between the two. During prayer you most likely are asking a higher power for guidance or help during a difficult time in your life. In meditation, these questions are also asked, but you take time to offer thanksgiving, and then sit quietly to listen for the answers all with the understanding and trust that everything will be revealed when the time is right. It is taking a few minutes to be patient, and open to receive what it is you have asked for.

Some people use a daily meditation practice on their personal journey of enlightenment by creating a oneness with nature, the Universe, and Spirit. Others will use it simply as a form of relaxation in order to rid their mind and body of negative and stressful emotions. Both are equally important to developing focus, inner peace, and well-being, to your mind, body, and spirit. Finding and holding onto this centre is vital in manifesting what you desire, uncovering your path and purpose, and opening your intuition. It is through this practice that you will find you become more in tune with your own emotions, ego, and physical body, and you will develop the ability to clearly see your purpose. A calm and centred spirit and mind will bring peace by releasing stress, and this in turn heals emotions and the physical body. Once you feel less stress and pain, you are able to then focus on moving forward.

By incorporating the exercises in the previous chapters in a meditation, you can truly feel and see things manifesting in your life. It all starts with letting go of the fears and stresses that are holding you back, and meditation is the perfect tool to help you.

Choosing a meditation technique that fits your personality, life style, and present needs, is your first step in developing this practice. If you don't feel comfortable, both physically and emotionally, you are not likely to follow it through. Meditation does not need to be rigid and precise unless you are the type that does better with a lot of structure and discipline. The only thing to watch for with this is that you don't get in the habit of paying more attention to the technique, and less to your intent.

Remember the purpose of your meditation is to bring peacefulness to your mind, body, and spirit, so you can heal the emotions and body, visualize what you wish to manifest, embed your positive affirmations, and above all to be in the present moment. As a result clarity and focus can be obtained.

Guided Meditation

Especially when you are first starting to meditate, you may find a guided meditation is the easiest to use. By listening to either a recorded meditation, or better yet, taking part in a group meditation led by a facilitator, you will find your breathing and visualization is directed in such a way as to take you to a certain place and time. You are better able to close out the world around you as you listen to soothing music, and the voice of your leader. Should you get distracted, you can always bring your awareness back to the facilitator, and you then find yourself drifting back into deep relaxation.

There are many recordings on the market today. It is best to start off with ones that are not too lengthy, then progress to more advanced meditations as you become more familiar with the routine. Guided meditations that involve what is known as grounding at the beginning, usually through deep breathing, assist you in strengthening your own awareness to your body. In this way you will find you are able to better recognize signs of stress, and then release it through your meditation. Guided meditations are usually done with a specific intent for spiritual growth, manifesting, releasing fears and negative emotions, and improved health, just to name a few topics.

Walking Meditation

Should you be one who enjoys being outside and moving around, the walking meditation would be a wonderful way for you to begin your practice. Obviously, you are not going to close your eyes and attempt to wander around the woods or parks, but rather you are heading out on a slow, focused walk, where your steps and breath are working together. The objective in a walking meditation is to head out without a destination or time to get there, but to simply open all your senses to the world around you, and become aware of the *now* moment.

- You begin by focusing your attention on your breathing by taking long, slow breaths in and out, allowing a set number of slow steps per breath. It will not be long before you develop a rhythm, almost a dance, between your movement and your breath.
- At this point, you can begin repeating your affirmation over and over again until it too becomes one with your breath, your step, and your intent.
- Next you can take time to see how many colours you notice in a tree, the grass, and the sky.
- Then do the same with scents. Can you pin point each individual scent in the air that you are breathing in?
- What about the sounds? What do you hear at first? Break it down as much as you can.

This form of meditation can also be done while walking a labyrinth (a sort of maze which is used as an aid for learning about the spiritual path—a symbol of your personal journey to finding your centre), or even indoors where room permits.

Other Methods of Meditation

There are many other ways of introducing meditation into your day. Many like to use sounds such as singing bowls, drumming, or chanting. There is the ancient form of meditation of repeating silently to yourself a particular mantra, which can be a single word, or a small group of words to assist you in relaxing and manifesting. In a way, when you use the affirmation you have written in your meditation, you are using it as a mantra. By repeating it over and over again throughout the mediation, it will become weaved into your subconscious mind.

Whether you decide to go it alone, join a group, or head to the park and walk it through, the important thing is to start. Go in without judgment of yourself, or of what you have to achieve, but rather allow the experience to happen. Remember it is the intent that is important. Do not worry if you are doing it right, long enough, or at the right time of day or night….at least not in the beginning. Your aim is to allow yourself at least 15 minutes a day to really spend time with the most important person—YOU! Creating your reality begins in your mind. How you feel about yourself, your goals, and meditation, is the perfect tool to get the creative juices flowing.

You are worthy and deserving of the time and energy it takes to make changes in your life. If you don't do this for yourself, I can guarantee no one else will. Do you think you are being selfish? Perhaps you don't have the time because you have family, friends, and work to deal with? Guess what? If you don't look after yourself first, you will be in no shape to help others. Think of all the time you may presently spend watching TV, movies, or searching the *World Wide Web*. This is time that could be used empowering yourself! Do you really need to watch another repeat of Seinfeld or Gilligan's Island?

Connecting to a Higher Vibration

"In a universe made out of energy, everything is entangled; everything is one." ~ Bruce Lipton

There was a time when men considered themselves to be a solid physical matter with the brain running all their decision making, and survival skills. As time has moved forward, they now realize there are fewer differences, and one huge thing that between man and animal, the earth, sky, water, and wind, are in common.... energy. Your body is composed of trillions of individual cells working and growing, ever changing to create the illusion that you are a solid mater. Medical and scientific researchers are now studying the invisible communication between these cells, or the vibration and frequency that they use to communicate with one another. After all, how do the cells know when to divide? When to heal? When to die?

Meditation has been one of the topics studied as science now can see that the intention of one's thoughts greatly affects their overall well being, and the vibration of your cells. This in turn creates a positive and healthy environment, or it can cause illness and depression. This all depends on your thoughts.

Everything has a vibration such as your body, your thoughts, things, people around you, and everything beyond the physical world. You *are* energy! By learning to focus on raising your own vibration to one that can manifest change, you are transforming your own energy into something more positive and beneficial to you. It starts with becoming more aware of your own physical body, your thoughts, and your desires. What you think, you become, what you put out, you attract. In time your own intuition will become sharper, and open to endless possibilities that previously you would have overlooked.

Breath Work

One of the easiest ways to move your energy is by breathing exercises. So much can be accomplished simply by learning to control your breath. Your body is designed to inhale purifying oxygen, and to release toxins and chemicals that do not serve your well being. As well, when you exhale, the muscles in your physical body relax, or they will if you bring awareness to doing just that. Since emotional stress is stored in your joints and muscles, you are also releasing stress that has been stored in your body from a disagreement earlier that day, regrets and anxieties from years ago, or worry about the future.

Your ancestors were no doubt deeper breathers than you are today. Back when everyone worked and played more outside, they would naturally be breathing in fresh, clean air. Today you will likely find you are in front of a computer, TV, or simply inside more than you are outside. Even when you are, do you work hard, or play hard? That would cause you to take in long, slow, deep breaths. Because the earth's air is more polluted than it was even twenty years ago, you need to take in more breaths to receive the amount of pure oxygen needed for optimum health. The more aware you become of your breathing, you will find you become more in touch with how it affects your moods, your relaxation, and your ability to focus and think with more clarity.

When used in meditation, deep breathing assists your physical body to relax, your conscious mind to quiet down so that your subconscious mind can be open to heal, re-program, and accept your positive suggestions. It is through breath work that you can move your energy, transform it so that it will draw more of what you desire into your life. You can begin the healing process by first becoming aware of your own body through breath work. Remember, you have all the tools you need inside you right now at this very moment, to begin the change process, and it is as simple as breathing.

Visualization

Now that you have your physical body relaxed, and realize you can quiet the mind by focusing on your breath, it is time to put into your mind's eye the image of what it is you wish to manifest. Remember, first you must conceive the idea of what it is you wish to obtain, and then imagine what it will be like to reach your goal. Imagine what it will, not only look like, but feel like. When you set this image in your mind during meditation, you are programming your subconscious mind, and in turn this thought will become your reality, replacing one of those repeated thoughts from the past that no longer serve you. Wouldn't you rather have your own thoughts from this present moment shaping your tomorrow instead of ideas perhaps based on fears from your yesterdays, or even worse those ideas of someone else creating your reality?

Everyone can visualize. As children you did it all the time when you imagined being a super hero, or during role playing in the school yard. As adults you call it a day dream, where you allow your thoughts to wander. This time, you will be focusing what you visualize on what it is you wish to manifest. It is not only what you can "see" but how that thought makes you *"feel"* that is important. Everyone will visualize a bit differently, depending on the outcome they desire, what their present fears are, and if they allow outside influences to shape their ideas. When you visualize, do so without fear, with the knowing that anything and everything is possible. What if instead of thinking something was *"impossible",* you took that word and changed it into *"I'm possible"*. You see, it is all how you look at it! After all, it is your imagination that gives you the ability to create. Where would we be if individuals didn't take the step out of what was accepted today and allow their imagination to create works of art, advances in medicine, to evolve spiritually, or become leaders for others to follow?

Now that you are ready to visualize, it is equally valuable to find ways to hold onto your vision. In today's world it is so easy to become side-tracked and swayed away from your own thoughts. Like your dreams that slowing fade away with the morning light, your visions you created in your mind's eye can vanish if you allow other ideas to over shadow them. Keeping a journal is an excellent way to create a contract with yourself by recording your goals, your thoughts, and desires. Once you write something down, it actually becomes more etched into your subconscious mind, and in turn will more quickly develop into your reality.

Stress filled days, Sleepless nights

When you are under stress it is hard, if not at times impossible, to believe you are capable of manifesting anything in your life. It all goes back to a fear of something, or allowing your ego to take over. When this happens self-doubt, anger, and discouragement, often step in and take up your precious thought space. Meditation is the most beneficial way to release stress in your mind, body, and spirit. Is it easy? Sometimes it can be very hard to sit and focus on something or nothing, but if you do, you can feel the victory of controlling your destiny right away. It has been proven that as little as 15 minutes of meditation is equal to 3 hours of deep sleep to your body. That doesn't mean to give up sleep, but what it does mean is that if you are struggling to relax your body and mind spending those precious 15 minutes for you can make a huge difference in how you look at the world. Your body will thank you by releasing the tension in the joints and muscles so you can focus on what you desire, and not on the aches and pains. You will feel refreshed, and the ego will just have to take a back seat as you begin visualizing what you desire, and thinking in a positive manner once again. Can't sit still? That is okay because now you know to do your deep breathing during a walking meditation so that you bring your awareness to the world around you, and the breath of life moving through you.

Create a meditation practice, and soon you will find that you not only feel more focused throughout your day, but you will begin to rest better at night. Too often when your mind is running every which way with worry, fear, and anxieties of all shapes and sizes, sleep will escape you. By meditating an hour before bed, you will relax your mind and body so you can focus on your sleep, instead of everything else. It is best to create a bedtime routine for yourself as your subconscious mind will soon associate your rituals with going to sleep, and this will assist your body in following along. Here are a few simple steps to take in order to unwind before bed:

- An hour or two before going to bed, find a quiet and comfortable spot where you can sit or lay down to meditate. Make this your time, and be clear to everyone not to disturb you! You deserve this time to relax. No phones, TVs, or computers, unless to play a meditation recording or soft relaxation music.
- Use whatever form of meditation you like for at least 15 minutes, or longer. It is better if you do not fall asleep as you don't want to sleep every time you meditate, but should this happen, that is okay too.
- After you meditate, take a few minutes to record in your journal anything that may have come to you, how the meditation made you feel, etc.
- Make yourself a hot cup of herbal tea or lemon water, but no caffeine or alcohol as these will keep you awake.
- If you are an evening bather this would be a good time for soak in the tub or a long shower. Definitely put on something cozy.
- It is best not to watch any violent shows, movies, or the news before going to bed. Should you wish to read, keep it light so that you are not dreaming about what you just saw on TV, or read!

- No more computer or cell phones. These give off microwaves, which will keep you up! Besides, you have just relaxed your body and mind, so why stir things up again? Never have the cell phone under your pillow, or on the bedside table.
- When you go to bed, have your room as dark as possible, and the temperature should not be too hot.
- Still a bit restless? Once in bed take deep breaths, and bring your awareness to various parts of your body, relaxing the muscles as you exhale. Soon you will be in lullaby land.

Awareness and Intention

Everything around you is a result of a choice you made. At the time you may not have felt you had any options, but a choice none the less was made by you. How you act and react to someone else's decisions and actions is totally and completely up to you. You can be encouraged by someone's words or feel broken and defeated, but it isn't their words that are hurting you, but rather your own acceptance of them that is building you up or tearing you down. Your thoughts are creating your reality.

What is it you want to focus on? Manifesting what you desire, or leaving your future up to someone else? It will come down to where you place your intention. So what is the difference between awareness and intention, especially as it is used in meditation?

It all comes back to everything and everyone being composed of energy, and as such, you are constantly transforming. By changing how you think, you put into motion changes in your physical and emotional body, which in turn will begin to influence the energy and information of your extended body. This is when manifestation is born. Think of intention as the field of unlimited potentiality that has the ability to transform your thoughts into your reality. When you have an idea, a desire you wish to manifest, it is like planting a seed in this wonderful field of endless possibilities. Your intention is the desire for this seed to take root and grow. Your awareness is what feeds and nurtures the seed, and in time it begins to transform your idea into your reality. Wherever awareness goes, intention grows. You could think of awareness as the fertilizer for our intention garden, which is the food for your manifestation.

By taking time to be more aware of how your body feels at this moment in time, or the energy of the space around you, whether you are outside in nature or in a crowded room, you will be prepared to notice a shift in this energy. By raising your awareness in all five of your senses, you will then be more open to make things happen in your life, because now, your sixth sense will have become more in tune as well.

Sixth Sense

Believe it or not, everyone has a sixth sense, but like everything else, if you don't bring your awareness to it, and allow yourself to use it, you lose the ability to "know". Your intuition is what makes it possible for you to be warned of approaching danger by sensing the negative energy of a person or place. Have you ever gone into a room and instantly felt uneasy despite the smiles on the people's faces? This often is the case if you have just walked into a space after a big argument, and those involved are attempting to cover it up. If you are a parent, you have undoubtedly been met with your children's angelic faces, only to discover a bit of mischief had just taken place. It is your intuition, or sixth sense, that senses the energy. Through meditation, you learn to be aware of whether this energy is positive or negative, and how you need to react to it.

By raising your vibration, you are able to manifest more quickly as you open your intuition to receive awareness to opportunities that can help you on your journey. This trip is not meant to be met with continuous obstacles. If that is what is happening to you, perhaps you need to rethink your plan, change courses, and really listen to what your sixth sense is trying to tell you! After all, through mediation, you are putting out to the Universe what it is you desire, so now is the time to be willing to receive the opportunities they present to you. Learning to trust those *"gut"* feelings can take some practice, as you need to discern between Universal guidance, and your ego.

Synchronicity

Definition*: the simultaneous occurrence of causally unrelated events, and the belief that the simultaneity has meaning beyond mere coincidence.*

Have you heard the expression, "Everything happens for a reason"? This would be the simplest explanation of synchronicity. It is the belief that there are no coincidences because that implies things happen by chance, without purpose or meaning. Often it is hard to define the purpose of an event while it is occurring, especially if it involves tragedy, but if you step back and look objectively to see what led up to the event, and choices you now have as a result of this, you can see how it fits into your life's puzzle. Simple things like meeting, hearing, or reading, about a key person, event or place that you need to further your desire. Perhaps bumping into an old acquaintance you haven't seen in years, only to discover they are an important link to an idea you have. Maybe you are being offered an unexpected opportunity. Even having a door close to what you at first thought was something you wanted, only to find it was needed in order for another more meaningful door to open for you. When you are more open to receive messages from the Universe your awareness is then placed fully on manifesting what you desire. You will trust these meetings, opportunities, and changes, that are necessary to further your journey.

Take a few moments to journal events in your life to date. Make a time line in the following way:

- Try to do so without emotion at first, but simply brief facts such as; I started kindergarten, went to church, started my first job etc.
- Then go back and in a single statement write how this impacted your life at that time.
- Now write a second statement through your eyes of this moment as objectively as possible, stating how this shaped your life choices. Can you see your part in how you allowed it to make you feel? The choices you made?
- Can you see how each step shaped where you are now? Take away the blame of others or situations, but rather look

for a positive lesson you learned that can help you today, and into the future.

Don't be surprised if this takes a few attempts. It isn't easy to do a life review, as it will no doubt stir up old emotions. Don't worry, you will deal with releasing in the next chapter. For now write down what it is you desire for your future, and see if you can find past life lessons that will help you to reach this desire. Perhaps you went through a life experience that was emotionally painful for you at the time, but from that you learned you have the inner strength to move forward and be a survivor, not a victim of circumstances. You are here today with the opportunity to start fresh, with more determination, and the tools of mind, body, and spirit. You'll have the strength to achieve more than you could ever have imagined.

Benefits of Meditating

Meditation is a personal experience between your mind, body, and your Higher Self, or spirit. It connects you to your own being, the earth, universe, and the Divine of your understanding. Whether you are looking for a spiritual experience, ways to distress your life, or a method to bring life changes, meditation is the most important stepping stone you can use. Here are just a few of the benefits you can find when you introduce meditation into your routine:

- Over all stress release from the body.
- A more relaxed feeling, which in turn relieves physical, and emotional pain.
- Emotional healing.
- More focus on daily tasks.
- Feeling of personal control over your own destiny.
- Forgiveness of yourself, and others.
- Ability to see a pattern in your life, and ways to learn from it, or change it.
- Manifesting your desires.
- Release of negative emotions, such as anger, sadness, or self doubt.
- Gathering positive emotions of love, compassion, forgiveness, and hope.
- Over all well being, and a positive outlook on life in general.
- No matter what is going on around you, there will be an inner peace, and a place of calm that you can go to in order to regroup and strengthen yourself.
- On a spiritual level, you will find you are receiving messages of love and guidance.
- You may even begin to experience glimpses into previous lives that will help to show you patterns to avoid or explore.

Ready to Meditate?

Many people have never even attempted meditation because of preconceived ideas about where they need to be to meditate, how to go about it, or tried it once and decided it did nothing. As with all things worth doing in life, patience and practice are key to a meaningful meditation practice.

As described previously, you can be in a room alone, meditating with a group or walking in nature. The most important thing is your intention to relax, cut off the outside world so you can connect to your inner voice, release stress, be open to visualize what it is you desire, and with practice, hear and see what it is you need to do next. In this busy technical world it is extremely important to literally unplug from everything. That means no TV, computer, or phones, running in the same space. The only exception would be if you are playing soothing relaxation music or a guided meditation, but no rock and roll, text messaging, or email alert alarms, going off. This is your time for YOU! Make yourself comfortable, either sitting or laying down. You may wish to have a shawl or blanket as your body temperature will change during meditation. Some get hot while others feel cooler. Others may like the comfort of a shawl.

Anytime that you can be in this space is good, but meditating as soon as you get up in the morning, before your day begins, helps you to reinforce your goals and intentions. Then again in the evening works best as you can give thanks for the day, and again place your intentions in your subconscious for the future. It also will help you get a good night's rest. Remember, you are manifesting your reality, and that is rather important, isn't it? If you were told to be early for work, you would no doubt set your alarm, and get up in time to get there, so isn't it even more important that you set time for you? After all you are worth it!

Are you ready to get started? Here are a few helpful steps to get you started for a private meditation in your home.

- As mentioned, select a quiet, private place where you will not be disturbed.
- Be sure to have no phones, TV, or computers, unless you are playing a guided meditation or relaxation music. HINT: Do not play music where someone is singing/playing your favourite rock and roll or country tune as your mind will want to sing along. Instead, select instrumental or nature type music designed for meditation or spa type settings. This will quiet your mind, and relax your body.
- If you are someone who finds it hard to quiet your mind, then a guided meditation recording would work best for you. They tend to use breath work and visualization to keep you focused.
- Some like to dim the lights, light a candle, smudge, or have incense burning, to create a soothing and sacred space. Do what is comfortable for you. As your mediation practice increases, you may find you want to introduce a variety of rituals, or cut some out…whatever you find is best for you, is what you should do.
- **Never meditate where your conscious mind is needed!!** This is not the time to multi task, so no meditating while driving, using heavy equipment, or machinery, please!

- Allow at least 15 minutes for your meditation. Longer is always good.
- Should something happen, you are really pressed for time, even doing your deep breathing can bring a sense of peace and calm to your overall well being, and this can be done anywhere, any time.
- Begin by taking at least 5-6 very long, deep, slow breaths in through your nose, then exhale slowly out through your mouth. Focus solely on your breath. This will help to slow down your breathing, your heart rate, and bring focus inward.
- If during your meditation, you find your thoughts are wandering, bring your awareness back to your breath, being mindful of its gently going in and out.
- Move your awareness throughout your body, relaxing the muscles with every exhalation.
- Allow yourself to just be in the moment. If you are visualizing, now would be the time to see in your mind's eye what it is you are manifesting. Remember to see it, and above all feel it, as though it has already happened, then allow that feeling to fill every cell of your being. It is the emotion that will remain with you, so make it as positive as you possibly can.
- During your meditation give thanks for anything and everything in your life. Those days where you find it difficult to think of even one thing, give thanks that you are able to be meditating!
- Ask to release all things that no longer serve you, and truly be willing to let things go.

- Ask to receive positive events, opportunities, and emotions, into your life.
- Repeat your affirmation with conviction.
- Bring your awareness back to your breath, becoming aware of your physical body once more.
- When you are done meditating, sit quietly for a minute or two in order to bring your conscious mind back to the space.
- Record your experiences in a journal

The more you do this as a daily practice, the more your subconscious mind will set this practice as a trigger, so that when you breathe deeply, your body will automatically begin to relax. The same goes for any ritual you use in your meditation practice. For example if you like to play certain music, light a candle, and wear a shawl. You will find that in time just doing these things will start your mind and body into relaxing. How wonderful is that?

Journaling

When you are first starting your meditation practice, you may have times when you wonder if anything is actually happening at all. The best way to monitor this is to keep a personal journal. These recordings are for you alone to see where you are at this moment, where you came from, and what your plans are for the future. Your goals will become your reality, the more you commit to them. It starts with you thinking of what you want, visualizing it in your mind's eye, saying it out loud, and writing it down. You are making a living contract with yourself and the Universe, when you do this. As you go through your meditation journal, you can see if you kept your promise to meditate daily, repeat your affirmation, and if you received a knowing, did you follow through? No doubt you will notice each one was a bit different in how you felt, if you were able to concentrate, or if you drifted off into the void, the place of nothingness where total connection to mind, body, and spirit, is held. It is also beneficial to record anything that may have occurred prior to, or after your meditation such as synchronicities that are helping your manifestation. Here are a few tips for your journal:

- Record the date and time of your meditation
- What type of meditation did you do?
- If you used an affirmation, record it here.
- How did you feel before, during, and after the meditation?
- Did you see anything? Hear or smell anything? (Hey, it happens!)
- Did you feel restless or calm? Energy moving through you will often cause a feeling of restless legs, or slight twitching. Ride it out as it is a good sign that things are moving, releasing, and letting go.
- If you have insight into something you should do, change at this moment, or if during the day or days ahead this happens, be sure to record it so you can see the connection.
- It is your journal, so record anything at all. There is no right or wrong. These pages are for you to use to vent, ask questions, and receive answers.

Chapter Six:

Letting Go

"When I let go of what I am, I become what I might be." ~Lao-Tzu

Do you feel stuck, out of focus, or completely at a loss as to what to do next? Perhaps you are in a place of confusion, where on one hand, the world seems to be quickly passing you by, and on the other, you feel trapped in the repetitiveness of everyday tasks. You want out one minute, but are afraid to move the next. It is far too easy to become absorbed in the mundane and lose focus of what it is you want in your life. You may know in your heart you need to change, yet you continue to do the same thing over, and over again, only to become more frustrated. But then, how can you expect things in your life to change, if you continue the same old patterns? If you have changes, what you are doing outwardly, but still feel stuck, perhaps you need to investigate what is going on in your thoughts. Are you holding onto ideas, emotions, or memories, which are blocking you from moving forward?

Often it is your own thinking that is stopping you. Fear and ego question your motives, your actions, and create unrest and impatience. Reminding yourself that things work in Universal time, and not necessarily in the order you think is best, will assist you into easing into a new reality. If you find you are slipping back into the old way of thinking, you have the ability and power within yourself to start over again, to retrain the brain, and start seeing the opportunities that surround you. The only limits are the ones you build around yourself.

By remembering that 95% of your thoughts are reruns, you will be able to recognize an old thought pattern. That is why it is essential to objectively look at your life, then and now, to see what you may be repeating. Not all patterns are harmful, but are they creating the results you need today? They may have served you well twenty years ago, or even last week, but will they generate a new result today? Are these ideas and actions true to you, or are you following someone else's life in the hopes that it will bring you joy in your own? It is very helpful to learn from example, but at some point you will best serve yourself by listening to your own thoughts and heart to uncover your personal joy. That is what meditation can bring into your life; a place of purpose for you alone.

Back in chapter three, you learned about fears, and how they stop you from moving forward. If you feel now that you are still stuck, then it is definitely the time to dig a little deeper, and find out what your root fear really is. It is certainly not uncommon to think you have everything all figured out then smack, you hit another wall. Changing your thoughts and manifesting in your life is often like peeling away layers upon layers of old ways of doing things, negative thought patterns, and past memories, in order to get to the core, the essence of what you need to overcome. Covering up the fear will not make it go away. In fact, it is much like covering up a weed with dirt. If you don't pull out the weed, and take it out of your garden, all you do when you bury it with earth is make it root even deeper, multiply, and grow. Your thoughts are tucked away in your subconscious mind covered in excuses, emotions, and often regrets, until one day when you go to reach for something else, it pops up stronger than ever, and takes over your thoughts. However, if you pay attention to your thoughts, and your emotions, you can face the fears, uproot them, and throw them away for good. You have to acknowledge them, to release them.

All of your memories and thoughts come down to two categories of either something that brings us pleasure, or pain. You are the one who selects which thought will be associated with which emotion, and you are the only one who can change that selection. By looking at your past through objective eyes, those filled with self love and learning, rather than judgment, you will realize there are no wrong experiences, but rather life lessons. You cannot go back and change the past, but you will do it justice by learning from it. What positive life lesson did it teach you? That particular event may have had an impact on your future actions and responses. but it does not need to determine who you are at this moment in time, or who you are to become in the future. Believe that you were acting the best you knew how at a particular moment in time. Like everyone else on this planet you have said and reacted in a way you now wish you could change. If you now admit your participation in the result, then you can change how you react today, and tomorrow, in that way you have learned a valuable life lesson. You can stop the pattern from repeating.

One of the hardest things about letting go is that you will most likely need to remember it in order to get rid of it, and this can often cause an uncomfortable feeling. Your mind is funny that way. You need to remember in order to forget. For example if you were told whatever you do, don't think about purple elephants. What is the first thing that happens? Your subconscious mind goes looking for an image of a purple elephant, and produces it in your mind's eye. Then the next step would be for your conscious mind to tell you not to look at it, so *"pop"* away it goes. Now that you have gone through those steps of remembering, then programming your mind to forget, you will be able to not think about purple elephants in the future, or at least not with the same emotion attached.

You can of course, simply ask in meditation, and in your affirmation, that you release all things that no longer serve you, and often this will release deep rooted memories. However, there are those memories and ideas that seem to haunt you, and influence your actions and for whatever reason you choose to hold onto a corner of that hatred, that sadness, that bitterness, loneliness, or indecision. Perhaps you want to have something to blame if you do not succeed, but then you are giving in to your fear of failure right? What if you simply lined up your fears, your negativities right there in front of you, and then had the power to release them? Otherwise, your fears are apt to pop up when you least expect them when triggered, and up comes the blockages again.

Objective Viewing

Depending on your past memories, it can be very difficult to sort out your fears and make changes. There in can lie a fear of discovering what the root fear really is. In certain cases it would be in your best interest to seek out professional help in clearing as the emotional attachment may be very strong. By having someone guide you through the process, it may actually keep you on track. This is often true in cases where there has been physical and psychological abuse as a child. However, even if you are receiving help, how you work through this will be up to you. By learning to detach yourself emotionally from the memory as you are viewing it, will help you see what was really going on. If you were a child, you can remind yourself that you are no longer a child, and see the situation through adult eyes. Often this is necessary to remove undeserved guilt and remorse. You may ask yourself questions such as:

- What else was going on in my life at that time? Were there circumstances, or situations that were out of my control because of my age, finances, or inexperience?
- Would I react the same today?
- If I could go back in time, what positive words of encouragement could I give myself? To others involved?
- Even if this event was extremely difficult at the time, what strength, power, or positive lesson, can I take away from it? Even if it is just to say you are here now!
- Did this create patterns for me today? Are these patterns helpful?
- What fear did this create, or what positive habit did it make for me today?

If you continue to do things exactly the same as you did in the past, you will always be in the past. The future will always seem out of reach, and today will be spent thinking about yesterday, and either living in fear, or in denial of your purpose and path.

Living in the past holds you back from manifesting in your life *because* (now you have read this a few times already but really listen this time!), your thoughts create your reality. If you are always thinking about your past, you are not planting any new ideas in that wonderful field of endless possibilities, and all that awareness goes to yesterday! It would be like harvesting your garden, but not taking the time to sort through your stock from last season to separate the spoiled fruits from the good ones. Instead, you throw them altogether, then wonder why everything goes bad! When you don't sort out your thoughts, and continue to keep the entire negatives from yesterday, soon your thoughts are over come with spoiled thinking! Now is the time to clean out the storage bins to make room for the new harvest of wonderful, positive, and creative ideas!

What if you were to look at your life as though it were one huge jigsaw puzzle with thousands upon thousands of pieces to choose from? Now, imagine that every piece of the puzzle is a memory, idea, or life event that has happened thus far. It may even be that you have pieces here from past lives, this life, or even bits of what is yet to come. By picking up one of these pieces, can you see how the choices that were made brought you to where you are today? Can you put together the synchronicities of these events and see what part you played in the choices that were made? What pieces can you choose from today to direct where you want this life puzzle to lead you? This is an exceptional puzzle as you hold, literally in your hand, the deciding pieces. The picture that is created is all up to you. You can continue to go along the path of the past, and the picture will not change at all from yesterday, or you can begin switching things around, and design a whole new and unique pattern; something that fits you alone.

It is so much easier to look back, and see how things could have been done differently, but don't be too hard on yourself. Remember, you are a different person today than you were then, and so is everyone else. The choices you made yesterday were decided by you with what you felt at that moment in time, which was the best thing to do, but that doesn't mean you have to make the same choices today. Now that you have acknowledged your part in how you have arrived at where you are today, you are more than ready to make changes for your future.

Forgiveness

Forgiveness may appear to be the highest hurdle for you to jump over on your journey through life. Perhaps you were raised to forgive others in order that you should be forgiven by God or others, but maybe you were not taught how liberating it is to forgive yourself as well. Often you may find it easier to let go of the hurtful words and actions of others, than it is to forgive and let go of words and actions performed by you towards others. Perhaps you have thought something negative, said or done something hurtful towards another, and they are totally unaware of it. But you know, after more careful thought and examination of the situation, or as you move through your own awareness, you truly regret your actions. This regret, if not relieved, will begin to form blockages on your pathway. Added to this are the roadblocks formed by the actions of others that you have allowed to build up, and stops you from moving ahead.

So, what do you do to dissolve these blocks? Granted, it is not always an easy task, and may take many attempts. That is why you must always be open to forgive, and be forgiven. Remember, you always have a choice between accepting a grievance, or a miracle. Let go of the regrets, grievances, and remorse, and embrace the miracle and blessings before you.

The first giant step forward on this journey is to accept your part in allowing the past to hold you hostage to your fears. It begins by releasing the underlying self-centred fears that keep you angry, shameful, resentful, and filled with contempt for others, and yourself. This letting go is like taking down a wall of stones that is blocking your path. With every act of forgiveness, another stone in the wall is knocked down, and your intuition begins to see more clearly. The path to manifesting begins and continues with every stone that is taken away. Through this act, you allow your mind, body, and spirit, to focus once more on their unity, no longer ego driven, but guided by love and compassion. In other words, your intention can be nurtured by your awareness…*intention grows where awareness goes.*

Don't be surprised if just when you think you have taken down the last stones, another one emerges. Forgotten barriers will appear as your lives evolve, and you are ready to break them down in order to move forward with our inner growth. Intuition will blossom through forgiveness as only by forgiving others, and yourself, will love be able to grow.

In order to be free of the bondage of your fears, it will be necessary to let go of all self-righteous thoughts, and the need to continually wound yourself; to stop hiding behind the cloak of the victim, and the shawl of *poor me*. Only you have the power within to rise above any negative circumstances. These are in the past, and can only keep you captive if you allow the chains of these memories to hold you back from the joy of today. Once more you need to step high above yourself and see the bigger picture and the truth that everything has a purpose in your life. It is your task to learn the lessons from these events and people, who have entered your life. By releasing the hurt and regrets, you allow positive light to enter your life, and your intuition will become in tune with the Universe, and the Divine purpose.

What happens if you hang on to these hurts? You will not grow. You will find the shadows coming back into your life over and over again, repeating the patterns through you, while you in turn will end up passing these shadows on to others. You cannot expect to grow spiritually if you are fighting the inner shadows within yourself emotionally, and physically. You may fool yourself into believing these shadows are gone or forgotten, but they will be responsible for blocking your path throughout your life until you call them out, and face them. Thinking you have forgotten them is not the same as forgiveness. The choice is always yours to make the changes in your life. Why choose unhappiness, shame, anger, and hate? Let them go and allow yourself to be free from their chains, and truly soar!

- Be honest with yourself and see your flaws so that you may transform them in to positive actions.
- Be aware of how forgiveness can make you stronger, more ethical in your own behavior, or more understanding, and tolerant of others.
- Know that if you feel there is something you can never forgive, you are the ones who make it this way. Pray for the willingness and strength to forgive, otherwise it will hold you captive, and keep you a victim.
- You do not need to confront the person(s) when you are seeking forgiveness, whether it is yourself, or you are forgiving them. It is about making you feel better, fulfilled, and strengthened. They may not even feel they need forgiveness or why they should forgive you in either case you would be placing your forgiveness, and how you feel in their hands, not yours.
- For forgiveness to be affective, it must come from your heart, not just empty words.

Gratitude

Take a moment and think about how you start your day. Is it with a grateful heart, or one of worry and despair? You likely know you should be thankful, but within your heart do you truly feel it? It can be difficult to cut through all the negative energy around you, but by reminding yourself of all the many blessings in your life, you are able to cast off these negative feelings, and remove them from your aura, and in turn prevent them from developing into physical, and/or emotional disease. It is extremely hard to bring more abundance into your life if you are not already grateful for something you have already. How is the Universe supposed to know when you are thankful?

There are some easy steps you can take to ensure that you are being grateful each and every day. Here are just a few:

- When you awake in the morning, and immediately upon opening your eyes, say to yourself *"thank you"*. You have another new day to kick the can of life, so go at it with a positive attitude. Shape your destiny!
- Challenge yourself daily by trying new adventures. Try anything new, even if it is as simple as driving a different way to the store or work.
- Decide to give love to everyone you meet by way of a smile or a kind word. These cost nothing, but can mean so much, not only to you, but the one receiving your gift.
- Allow gratefulness to *become* a part of our being. Look out the window and see something amazing. Wait, if you can see it, isn't that amazing?
- A heart singing praises will not have room for any negative feelings, at least not for long. It's a choice you make to accept the positive feelings that come with gratitude, or to turn it away.
- Taking time to be grateful will open you up to be ready to receive the wonderful things the Universe has to offer you.
- The more grateful you are, the more will come your way. Remember the energy you put out is what will be attracted to you.

- Before going to sleep, think of at least five things you are grateful for. They can be the same as yesterday, big or small, new or old. Be sure to think of them. Of course, you can make your list longer if you like!
- Include thankfulness as part of your meditation.
- Write down in your journal what you are grateful for.

Remember that appreciation is a doorway into your heart, once opened it allows more love to flow through your life. By giving true gratitude, you are putting aside judgments—stepping outside of your head, and going directly to your heart. When you do this, the Universe is able to work more directly with and through you, and will bring you what it is you wish to manifest.

Meditation for Letting Go

Here is a guided meditation for releasing all that baggage you have been carrying around. Just as an over packed backpack can literally weigh you down, holding onto those thoughts that no longer serve you can do the same. Once you learn to let go of what you no longer need to carry, you will feel emotionally and spiritually lighter. By filling your backpack with love, forgiveness, and gratitude, it actually becomes lighter, and helps to lift you up. How does it get any better than that?

As with all meditations, find a spot where you will not be disturbed, create a sacred space if you wish with candles, incense and soft relaxation music. Make yourself comfortable, and close your eyes.

- Begin your meditation by taking five deep, long, slow breaths through nose, then slowly exhale through your mouth.
- Focus on each breath.
- With every breath imagine you are breathing in healing, positive energy, and exhaling any stress, and negative emotions. Feel the muscles in your body relax and let go.
- Bring your awareness down to your feet, and using your imagination, sense that you have roots growing out of the bottoms of your feet, going deeper, and deeper, into the earth.
- Feel the relaxation flow through your body as you connect to the calming energy of the earth.
- Imagine you are breathing up that peacefulness into your body.
- Now look up, and imagine a golden light flowing over your body, uniting you to the Universe, reminding you that you are endless possibilities.
- Now see and feel a soft white light surround you, making you very relaxed and calm. This is pure love protecting, and surrounding you now, and throughout the meditation.
- As you breathe in, you absorb this white light, and you now see you are on a pathway along a white sandy beach.
- In front of you is a large backpack and you can tell it is filled beyond being full! However you realize you are able to lift it up, and put it on.
- You begin to walk along the beach, at first admiring the beauty around you, and you give thanks for this.

- You then begin to feel how heavy the backpack really is. It becomes your focus, and not the beautiful beach. You find you are focusing more and more on the weight of the bag on your back.
- You continue on your journey until you cannot tolerate the weight any longer.
- You stop, and take off the bag.
- It is then you open it up and see that inside are all the pains, the memories from the past, the hurtful words spoken to you, and by you, the people and events that have caused pain in your life, or to whom you have caused pain. There may even be dark packages that you don't recognize because you have been carrying them around for so long.
- Also in your back pack is a small shovel. You take it out.
- You begin digging a hole as big as you need to bury your weights that are in this bag.
- Once you have the hole dug, begin taking out the packages and as you place them in the hole, look at them, thank them for the lesson they taught you, give forgiveness, and place it in the hole.
- Continue to do so until your bag is lighter or empty (You may need to do this a few times to really let go)
- Then fill the hole back in with sand from the beach.
- With every shovel full, say, "I am letting go of what no longer serves me"
- When all is complete, put the shovel back in your bag so you have it should you need to rid yourself of anything else.

- You put the backpack back on, and this time notice immediately how light it is, how light your heart is, and how much better you feel.
- Now you see the beauty all around you, and you continue your journey into the future as you see before you what you wish to manifest.
- You travel to meet your goal, allowing the feeling of accomplishment to spread through you with every breath.
- Slowly bring your awareness back to your breath, and your sacred space. Then open your eyes.
- Sit for a moment or two, reflecting on your meditation.
- Journal how this made you feel.

Chapter Seven:

Opening to Receive

"Your task is not to seek love, but merely to seek and find all the barriers within yourself that you have built against it." ~ Rumi

By now you should have the message that what you think will determine what you manifest in your life. How you feel about yourself will be how you present yourself to the world, and in turn how others look at you. To have others love you, first love yourself. To reach your goals, you must first know what those goals are, and what they mean to you. If you don't know, how is anyone else to know? If you don't know and simply let other people lead you, chances are they will be taking you down a path of their choosing, and not necessarily one that serves you well. When you put your intentions out to the Universe, make them as focused as possible. If this transmission from you is clear, then what you receive back will have more clarity and meaning.

Trusting that the Universe will provide, is huge in manifesting what you desire. Believing you are at the controls through your free will, and output of positive changing energy is at the core of manifestation. All around you, change is taking place by your actions, thoughts and those of others. Even when you feel nothing is going right, you could be at a changing point where your choices will be the deciding factor in how the events in your life play out. Remember that by always coming from a place of thanks giving, you are acknowledging to the Universe that you are able and willing to receive even more blessings into your life. Every trial makes you stronger. Every lesson learned makes you wiser. Every bit of forgiveness granted opens you for more love, and every heartfelt utterance of gratitude shows you are ready to receive.

When you truly trust that you are taken care of, and all is as it should be in this moment in time, you will then know that you are no longer living in fear. Oh, fear may creep back in every now and then, and have a chat with your ego to try and stop you, but now you know you can control your thoughts, and you have the tools to build yourself up and move forward. You can use your past experiences to teach you new ways of doing things so that you are not reliving the past mistakes, or repeating useless patterns. You can now be confident that your awareness is guiding you, and leading you into wonderful opportunities that it will be a better today, and even better tomorrow.

Sometimes you will need to attempt something a few times to understand that it is not the right path or journey for you at this moment in time. It could be through the trials and errors that you find the answers you are looking for. After all, the great inventors did not make their discoveries right away, but they did have a vision in their mind's eye of where they wanted to end up. They persevered, and followed their own intuition and purpose until they reached their goal. The same can happen for you. You may feel yourself sliding back to your old ways, but that doesn't mean you have to stay there. You are the master of your destiny, so why wait for someone else to come along! Grab your shovel of acquired wisdom, and life experience, and dig your way out!

Patience will be your greatest ally. It is something few humans seem to posses, yet it can be the most useful tool to own. Time was invented for man's convenience. Nature didn't need it as it instinctively knows that everything in the Universe moves and changes as it should, and when the time is right. The more you become in tune with your inner self, and the world around you, time will not be so important as you will learn to trust the Universe will provide for you, and things will happen when they are meant to. Don't be in such a rush, hurrying up to get to your destination that you miss the journey. There could other valuable lessons to be learned and opportunities that would better, benefit you along the way. Often things will move faster and smoother when you rely on your intent to be enough, and you use patience to wait for things to set into place. There are times when stillness will benefit you more than activity.

Remember that things do not always follow a straight pathway to your door. Take time to look around you, and be open to receive opportunities from people and places along your path. The Universe will often have someone or an event pop up that can introduce you to an unexpected way of doing things or meeting people who can help you. By simply being open to follow your sixth sense, you will find amazing things beginning to happen. There will be difficult times for sure. Unfortunately the ride is not void of bumps and turns, but if you remain focused and open, you will see the benefit of having weathered the storms that come your way. A word of caution: should you find everything seems to be stopping you from reaching your goal, you may be trying to paddle up that famous creek without a paddle, and the Universe is attempting to turn you around. At these moments it is good to take time out, reflect, regroup, and see if this is still the path you feel you need to be taking at this moment in time. What if where you are is exactly where you are supposed to be for now? What if you have some other lessons to learn before moving forward, so you can better handle what is ahead? It could be you need to take an alternate route, at least for the time being.

As you travel through this process, always look for what lessons you are learning? Be mindful of your actions and reactions, and know if they are coming from a place of love or fear. The more you live from love, the less stress you will feel, the more positive energy will be brought into your life, and the less anxiety you will feel about tomorrow. When you do fall, and it will no doubt happen on occasion, be gentle on yourself. Always pick yourself up, dust yourself off, and go at life again…even if you have to wait until the morning.

Making a Contract with Yourself

Back in chapter one, you were shown how to create a positive affirmation. It has been proven time and time again that those people, who not only think of what they want, but actually speak it then write it down, are more successful than those who do not. Using your journal to record your meditation, and keeping track of your feelings and synchronicities, is very helpful. Writing out your desires in the form of a positive affirmation takes it a step further. It is making a contract with yourself and the Universe and shows you are serious about the results, and committed to the cause. By having it written down where you will read it often, it acts as a reminder to place your awareness to this intention. This is especially useful in those times of chaos.

When you are writing your affirmation, you should be very clear in your desire using only positive words by focusing on what you want, not on what you don't want. Remember, you mind does not register negative words and places its awareness on what is left. Here is an example of what may appear to be a positive affirmation.

"I am overweight and starting today I will not eat anything with sugar or fat. I will not give in to bad habits."

Take a closer look at the above example. Keeping in mind how important the words used after *I am* can be as it tells you how you think of yourself. In this case you are defining who you are as someone who is overweight, but that isn't what you want to focus on. The second thing to consider is how your brain will store this information. Remembering that negative words will be omitted, you will now see the message your body is actually receiving from your brain,

"I am overweight and starting today I will ~~not~~ eat anything with sugar or fat. I will ~~not~~ give in to bad habits."

Hmm, not exactly the message you wanted to put out there is it? What if it were written this way:

"I am worthy of a healthy body. I am choosing to eat healthy foods. I am in control."

Here are a few tips in writing your own affirmation to be used as your personal contract:

- Write down what it is you desire.
- Go back and amend it by taking out any negative words or statements about what you do not want, and replacing it with words of encouragement, for what you do want, keeping it positive.
- Keep it short so it's easy to remember.
- Write it on a paper to carry with you. You may wish to post it where you can read it daily. This is private so you may not wish for everyone to see it unless you are all working on a common goal.

Remember to read and repeat your affirmation often, as this helps to program your thinking, and what happens when you do this? It becomes your reality. Once you have achieved this goal, work through the same process for your next goal. There is no end to what you can achieve and make manifest in your life once you start empowering yourself.

Chapter Eight:

Following Your Intuition

"Listen to your intuition. It will tell you everything you need to know." ~ Anthony J. D'Angelo

Once you make the decision to make things happen in your life, and follow the steps outlined in this book as your guide, you will find you are more in tune with your higher self, or spirit. After all, you are more than a body of water, blood, and bones, with a huge data base called a brain. You are a beautiful being of light who has decided to come to this little blue planet to evolve through all the experiences that life here can send your way. It is in those ups and downs that much strength and wisdom can be gained. Soon you are able to use this knowledge to map out your journey, using your intuition as your compass.

It isn't always easy to be aware of your spiritual self when you are constantly bombarded with incoming information from other energy sources such as radio, TV, the internet, and cell phones, just to name a few. More and more, you may find you are beginning to rely on electronic devices to communicate, to provide you with information, and to make life decisions for you, when really all you need to do is to be still, and listen to your inner voice. How else are you going to get to know that very important person in your life… you? Only you hold your own truth and understand what brings you joy. Now that you have taken steps to release your fears, there are no limits to what you can achieve.

Allow yourself to become aware of how your own energy feels around you and works through you. Then, when there is a change taking place, making the correct decision for example, you will be more in touch with your own sixth sense regarding the people and events surrounding you. It is very important to lose the fear of being wrong when it comes to learning to trust your intuition. The ego likes to step in and question whether what you are sensing is imagined, or the real deal. Push the analytical mindset to one side, and allow yourself to follow your intuition for awhile. In this way, you will learn how to differentiate between the intuition, and the ego. In a perfect scenario, you will be able to use both the intuition to guide you, and your conscious mind or intellect to set the plan in motion. If you don't take the leap of faith to use your intuition, you could end up remaining a prisoner of your fears and remaining in the same place, doing the same thing over and over again with no change in sight.

Through meditation you will find in the stillness the patience needed to really hear, feel, and understand your heart's desires. It is in this special and sacred space and time that you plant your ideas in that fertile ground of intention and through the repeating of your affirmations, nurture those ideas with your awareness. As you learn to remove the weeds of fear and self doubt, your intention will strengthen, your ideas will begin to manifest into your reality, and along with this your intuition will evolve as well.

Now this doesn't mean you will not make mistakes, become discouraged, or have to start over a few times. You are after all, a spiritual being in a human body, so you get to have all the emotional roller coaster rides that this life can hand you to experience, only now, you will find you look at things in a new and more positive way. When you can let go of holding onto what no longer serves you, a wonderful sense of freedom is born within you. You are able to focus more clearly on what it is you need to do, and when you kick ego out of your way, the path is more easily revealed.

One important thing to ask yourself, when you are working on manifesting your desires is, will this be a betterment for not only your life, but for that of others? Are the changes you plan on based on following your path with the desire to improve and better your life, and the lives of those around you, or is it rooted in fear, greed, and control? The Universe will assist you in meeting your goals if you come from a place based with motives that do not harm or put yourself or others in danger. If you feel you are constantly going against the stream of life, it is definitely time to re-evaluate your life plan, your motives, and how it affects, not only yourself, but those around you. It could just be it is not moving forward because your heart is in the wrong place. Power and control of others is a fear of losing control, and will only bring temporary glory if at all. Working from a heart of love will bring lasting joy and contentment. This is the path of your intuition.

The Five Questions

In the Hindu religion it is said that when you speak there are five gates that must be opened before your mouth opens to speak your words. Before saying anything, you should ask yourself five questions, and if the answer is yes to all five, then it can be said. These same questions can be applied when you are making a decision to act on anything in your life. By running these simple questions through your mind, and truthfully answering them, you will soon know where your desires are coming from. Is it love or fear? Is it the voice of intuition or ego that guides you?

- ***Is what I am about to say/do necessary?*** Asking this first question could very well stop you from putting one, if not both feet in your mouth! When it comes to manifesting, do you feel like this is a step that is required to set you on your path, or veer you away from your desires?
- ***Can it be said without hurting someone***? It isn't always easy to get away without someone else's feelings being hurt, or to meet everyone's approval. However, if you are doing or saying something to deliberately cause pain to someone, whether that is emotionally, or physically, you are working from fear. You cannot control how someone will respond to what you say or do, but you are responsible for the motive behind it.
- ***Is what I am about to say true***? Speaking from gossip, and with judgment is not speaking from love and truth. Follow your inner voice to speak your truth, and follow through with your actions, otherwise, what value do your words have?
- ***Can it be said in a kind and compassionate way?*** There are many ways to speak and act. If you take your time to think about what you say in a kind and compassionate way, you are showing you are taking into consideration the feelings of others. You can be truthful without being hurtful, to the point without appearing harsh, and strong

without being judgmental or controlling. All it takes is thoughtfulness, and really listening to what you are about to say. You can see what it is you're about to do objectively, and with the understanding of how it will affect your life, and others.

- ***Will this benefit the goal of higher good?*** Sometimes you can answer yes to all the above, but then realize perhaps this is not the time to bring up this subject or to act upon your thoughts. Often on your life's journey, there will be many times when you are wiser to remain silent, think things through, or act by yourself in order to move forward. There is a fine line between being afraid to step out of your comfort zone to achieve the higher good, and knowing the time is not quite right. Going back to whether you are responding from your intuition or the fear of the ego, will help you to decide the answer to this question.

Little Things are the Big Things

Normally in life, you are told not to sweat the little things, but when it comes to following your intuition, it pays to be aware of all the little things that happen in your life. It can be during a simple conversation with a complete stranger, which will give you a lead to further your journey. You may notice an advertisement several times in a row that could help you with a problem you have been having. Taking the plunge, and starting a new job or class can lead you to meeting someone, getting a phone number, or helping you gain insight and knowledge that will help you out even more.

By putting your desire out to the Universe for help, you must also be willing to receive the answers and these are often in forms you would not normally have expected. Keep your ears, eyes, and intuition open, and soon the little things will lead you to the big things. Sorting it all out is part of your amazing adventure to manifesting what you desire.

So far you have thought about what you want, felt it in your heart, meditated on it to put that positive energy out into the Universe. Now you are opening up to allow the return of positive results into your life. All that is left now is for you to sit back, and let it all work out for you, right? Wrong! Now, things can happen that quickly and easily, but usually you will need to take your thoughts, and put them into action. This is the next big step of faith.

Making a move, whether it is changing a job, relationship, or as easy as changing the colour of your socks, can all be challenging, depending on the place you are coming from, and that all goes back to releasing your fears. When you hold onto those fears, it is like putting blinders on, and you can only see what is right in front of you. These fears stop you from looking all around you, and sensing the opportunities that are within reach, if only you would look at them! It is important to remember that the Universe most often presents these opportunities to you in a roundabout way, not always the straight and narrow pathway you may be trying to see before you. If you are so caught up in things happening in certain order, or become impatient with the process, you may become discouraged, and good old ego will jump right in to take over the controls.

That is why flexibility is a vital companion to take along on your trip. It allows you to go with the Universal flow, and timing. Should you detour when you would have done better to keep on the path, flexibility will help you find your way back. Flexibility is a true champion as it will encourage you to keep going, help you get up when you fall, and learn life lessons in a grateful and positive way.

Life's Journey

Your whole life's journey is very personal and unique to you alone. Others will come and go, and together you will cross paths briefly, travel together until one of you takes a side street, and sometimes you will have a lifelong traveler, but in the end the experience is special to you. There may be times when you express how you feel, your desires, your hopes and dreams, or even confess your remorse and regrets to others, and they will listen, just as you listen to their life stories. However, only *you* really understand how you feel about all of these experiences, how they have served you, and what moves you are making next. Only you are in connection with your own intuition, feel your Higher Self connection, and know your purpose and path. You are the one responsible for the choices you make, the thoughts you have, and the lessons you learn. It is you, who will determine if you use your thoughts to create your own reality, or live in the shadow of someone else's dream.

The more you relax with the idea that you are a beautiful being of light, who has decided to experience a life in human form, the fears of actually getting out and experiencing life will fade away.

It is during this time of self discovery that you can open up your intuition to allow it to guide you, and bring things and people into your life that you never noticed before. They were there, yet you had not decided to acknowledge them. As you begin to trust your inner voice more and more, you will not only know what you want, but you will begin to draw it into your life and become what you want. You will soon walk in your own truth.

Learning to be aware of how you body feels through exercises to open your five senses more will in turn heighten your sixth sense as well. Follow through on a *"knowing"* you have, and see where it leads you. Have you ever taken some food in hand, and instantly thought, *"I probably shouldn't eat this"*, but did anyway? How often do you regret it? Your mind and body were working together to send you a message, but your power of choice decided to ignore it, then bingo...belly ache! Listen to the thoughts, and be aware of how your body reacts to certain ideas. That *"gut feeling"* is a sure sign something is not right for you. If you are considering taking a certain action, but feel conflicted about it, go through the five questions discussed earlier in this chapter, and be aware of how your body reacts. Is it a feeling of anxiety, tension, and negative responses, or is it one of happiness, excitement, and joy?

It is during your times of stillness such as meditation, walks in nature, or even soaking in the tub, that you connect through the silence to your higher self. It is in this place of nothingness that all your thoughts can be sorted out, your true desires created, and your fears released. It is only in the stillness that you can claim peace, and then move onward to focus and clarity. You deserve this time of self love. So often you will need to put out the intent, make a move, then quietly wait for the Universe to bring the actions into play. Impatience only creates discouragement and a feeling of despair, but trust that all is as it should be, and manifests what you desire with a sense of peace and contentment. Mind, body, and spirit, are united during your stillness, and it is through this connection that what you desire will happen.

Although you may experience many a troubled time along your life's path, you are not being punished, nor expected to go through life without pleasure and love. All things can come to you with ease, joy, and love, *IF* you first realize you are deserving of these things. You are energy, transforming with every breath into whatever you are meant to be. You can be what you desire to be. If your path is constantly rough it is time to sit by the roadside, and be still, while you review your directions.

- Are you finding time for the good and the beautiful in your life, and of your spiritual evolution, or are you running through each moment without a thought of the higher good?
- Are you remembering that your thoughts arc creating at least part of this reality? If there is drama, what part are you playing in it?
- Do you look for blessings and purposely give thanks for even the smallest of things in your life?
- Are you open to receive opportunities, and returned blessings when they appear to you, or are you travelling with blinders on, and missing all the helpful people, places, and events that are reaching out to you from all sides?
- Where are your thoughts? Do you see in your mind's eye

the possibilities that are before you, or only the obstacles you feel you have to overcome?

- Have you refused the Universe's guidance, and allowed your own ego to take over the controls? Perhaps you thought ego could get you there faster, only to find yourself stuck in the mud, and going nowhere. In your stillness, you can find your way back, if you only take the time to just *"be"*.

Instead of trying to go against the flow of the Universe, turn yourself around and allow it to guide you. It is much easier to row a boat with the current than against it, and so too with Universal timing. Your intuition is your connection and will take you to where you need to be.

Chapter Nine:

Stepping Out of Your Comfort Zone

The Comfort Zone – by anonymous

I used to have a comfort zone
where I knew I couldn't fail,
The same four walls of busy work
were really more like a jail

I longed so much to do the things
I'd never done before,
But I stayed inside my comfort zone
and paced the same old floor

I said it didn't matter
that I wasn't doing much,
I said I didn't care for things
like diamonds or furs and such

I claimed to be so busy
with the things inside my zone,
But deep inside I longed for
something special of my own

I couldn't let my life go by
just watching others win,
I held my breath and stepped outside
to let the change begin

I took a step, and with new strength
I'd never felt before,
I kissed my comfort zone good bye
and closed and locked the door

If you are in a comfort zone
afraid to venture out,

Remember that all winners
were at one time filled with doubt

A step or two and words of praise
can make your dreams come true
Greet your future with a smile,
success is there for you!

When you first read through the above poem, you may feel it is strictly about obtaining material wealth and gain, but in reality there is so much more to be discovered within these words. No matter what you go to do in and with your life, it is all up to you whether you take that first step to make changes in your life, how you perceive your present situation, and where you want to go in the future. Your life is what you make of it, and can be very easy to view your personal jail as your comfort zone.

How often have you said to yourself that you need to make a change? Either things cannot go on as they are, or you are simply unhappy in your present situation? Only you can initiate change in your life. If you continue to repeat the same patterns, then you are going to end up like the poor hamster running in circles in his wheel. At the end of the day you will still be in the same place you started out!

The comfort zone of words can be a bit misleading. It would seem to imply a place of contentment where you can be surrounded with that warm fuzzy feeling. True enough it could be, but more often than not it represents a place you can go where everything is familiar, and there are few surprises. Perhaps it should be renamed the *uncomfortable zone* as it is more of a prison than a home. You stay there because of the fear of the unknown. You may be living in a negative relationship because at least you know what triggers arguments, fights, or other forms of abuse, and you are afraid it might be worse *"out there"* or you are afraid of being alone and starting over . What if, instead of focusing on the entire negative "*what ifs*" the focus was placed positively on how your wings could be unfolded, and you were then able to fly? Staying in a job that you dread going to every day will bring stress to your mind, body, and soul, causing mental, and physical disease. What if you let go of the fear of being out of work, or not having enough, and replaced that with thanking this position as a stepping stone, and a learning experience for you to move forward? What if you thought of it as a way to keep you financially secure, while seeking out your passion?

Once you change your thinking, you will discover that it is you who holds the key, and only you, who has the power to use that key to open your prison door. Ultimately the choice is yours to make on whether you stay living in the past, or take a deep breath, and with your positive affirmation in your heart and mind, step into your future. Until you decide you are going to make a change, it will never happen. So what are you waiting for? Make today the day!

Moving Forward

So, you have made up your mind that things are going to be different, and you can see where you want to be. Now what? It can be as easy as not eating pizza every day, or walking to work, or even looking for a new job, but what if the change you need to make goes even deeper? Especially if you are dealing with matters of the heart, whether it is a relationship with someone else, a group of people, family, and even harder to deal with, love of yourself. There will no doubt be ties that will need to be cut so you can break free of your prison. These are not always easy as it can mean a physical distancing of yourself, or releasing past memories that are stored in that subconscious vault. But cut these cords, you must as they will keep you tied to the past, or in constant worry about the future. When you are focusing on the past, or what is yet to come, you are not in the present moment, and that is where your thoughts need to be in order to manifest what you desire.

Too often you may have allowed the words, actions and thoughts of others to influence how you think of yourself. This can result in self doubt, feelings of insecurity, or your own ability to make it in the world. However, these ideas can all be changed if you are ready to empower yourself. Start with the mindset that you, and you alone, are going to make a change. The only limits that surround you are the ones that you have placed around yourself, and only you can break them down. Instead of being afraid of this power, why not embrace it as your new strength and truth? Remember the children's story about the little train who got up the hill by saying, *"I think I can"?* Think how much more powerful and successful you will be as you escape your prison by thinking, believing, and saying, *"I am!"* You can move past wondering if you have the ability and courage to make changes, into truly believing in yourself and the Universe to create the opportunities now. To say you think you can make things different implies some doubt on your part, so instead, make it a certainty by saying, *"I am making changes"*, and live in the NOW!"

One of the most important things to remember is that you may need to take time to evaluate your progress. If you do not seem to be getting anywhere, or there are constant roadblocks, take time to see if you are allowing fear to lead, or if you need to take a different approach. It is not uncommon as you travel along your path that you will evolve to a new way of seeing and doing things, and you will benefit from changing your route. As you grow in mind, body, and spirit, it is only natural that your outlook on the world around you matures and grows as well. Give thanks for the life experiences, and take note on what you have learned so far, as this will lead you in a new and more beneficial way.

As you travel the road of your desires, you will find at times others will attempt to sway you into doing things their way, or talk you out of achieving your goals. If you allow yourself to place your success totally in someone else's hands, you are giving them your joy. You are responsible for your own happiness, and only you know what will truly make you feel as though you have reached your goal. Live your life for you, and the higher good, and you will succeed.

Equally important is for you to realize that just as you are traveling your own journey, others too are finding their path and purpose. Sometimes you will be in another's life to help them, or they will be there to help you learn a lesson. Just as you are not to allow others to control your thinking, you would do well to respect the ideas and actions of others. They too will need to find their own way, and their own truth. To guide them by example is one thing, but to try to take over and control them is definitely not beneficial to either one of you. Learning to listen, to work alongside others, to be empathetic to the world, and its people, are especially important tools to learn for those whose path is to be the leaders. It is one thing to be a coach and leader, and another to be a dictator, as one works from a heart full of love for the higher good of all, while the other thinks only of his/her power and control, thus working from a fearful heart.

Leaving your nest is made easier when you place your awareness and intent on your desires, then place your trust into the hands of the Universe and the Divine. All the time you spend worrying about making a mistake, taking the wrong turn, failing, or being too early, or too late, too smart, or not smart enough, is wasted time that you could have been using to put positive, motivated thoughts and energy into achieving your goals. This staying in the negative emotions of the past, and worrying about the future, only serves to create anxiety as you concentrate on all the what ifs and maybes. Around, and around, and around, your mind will go until finally you realize you are digging a hole instead of moving forward. Take a deep breath, make a decision, and lift those legs high, whether it is literally or figuratively, and step out of that comfort zone. You will instantly feel the anxiety melt away as it is replaced with clarity and motivation.

This moment in time is the only time you truly have. It is in this moment that you make your choice, choose your direction, and decide for yourself how you will act, or react to the situation around you. You are in control of your own soul's journey, so live in the experience you came to this earth to have. In doing so when your times comes to end this journey, and begin another, you will do so with few or better yet, no regrets, for you will have followed your intuition, and lived your passion with joy from a heartfelt place of love, not fear.

You now have the tools, the desire, and the help of the entire Universe, so what are you waiting for? How could you ask for anything more? Let your fears go, and get out there and experience life. The only wrong move, or bad experience, is not making a change, not taking a chance, and choosing to stay in your past. Don't be afraid to open those unfamiliar doors ahead of you, but rather throw them open with the expectation that behind each one lies endless possibilities for you to be all you can be.

Follow these steps, restarting if you have to, but never give up, never lose faith, because you can *Make it Happen*!

- Keep a journal that is written and read by only you. This is your record of what it is you desire, your fears to overcome, your acknowledgment of victories, and lessons learned from not so special moments. It is your personal contract with yourself to believe in you.
- Be sure to start each entry with blessings. No matter how difficult it may seem to enter anything positive into your journal, be sure to look deep in your heart, and find at least three things each day. Soon you will find that you have become filled with gratitude, and finding it everywhere, and in every new adventure that stretches out before you.
- Make note of all the synchronicities that happen, no matter how big or how small. Become aware of the pieces of your life coming together to form your desires.
- Practice daily meditation which includes a time of

gratitude, releasing of fears and visualizing your positive affirmations, and goals. See and feel yourself living the life you desire.

- Remember that all things begin with your thoughts. Conceive what you wish to manifest, then take that thought into your heart centre, and truly feel it as you believe it can be so. See it in your mind's eye, repeat your affirmation, and watch yourself achieve it in your life. Believe you are made up of limitless possibilities, and only you can break down the walls that hold you back from bringing joy and fulfillment into your life.

Love yourself first, believe you can do it, then step out of that comfort zone, and just do it! Soon you will wonder why you never realized this before.

Chapter Ten:

Time to Make it Happen

"The soul knows everything. Be who you are and your life will transform forever."~ Deepak Chopra

The fact that you have read this book means that at this very moment your soul has been awakened, and is ready to join in the Universal dance of manifestation. Perhaps this awakening has been brought on by some drama or trauma in your life, which has forced you to come face to face with the reality of a situation. No doubt you have had your own physical or emotional health shaken, or witnessed the well being of someone close to you jeopardized, or perhaps there has been an upset in your finances, restlessness with your job, unfulfilling relationships, grieving, or a feeling of disconnection to your personal spiritual growth. It may even be that you have become numb with the everyday routines you have gone through year after year without much pleasure or thought of how it could be changed.

Then it happens, finally, after years, you realize that all the complaining about your health, your job, and your present outlook, isn't getting you anywhere. There has been no knight in shining armour whisking you away, or fairy godmother waving a magic wand and making all things perfect and magical. So what happens now? You awaken to the truth that *you* are the one who can make change possible in your life, no...actually you are the *only* one who can make that change, and now you do it. It is just as simple, and as complex as that. You take that deep breath and begin believing in yourself and trusting in the Universe and the Divine to guide you. Now, having taken this first step, you must be prepared to meet head on the challenges and opportunities that await you.

Since you now know that everything begins with a thought, you can begin to recognize and accept that you need to believe you can, and will become the change you wish for in your life. No one can bring that to you, you alone have to create it. If you decide that you are never going to be happy again, it will not matter who you meet, where you go, or what you do, you will not discover happiness in your world. However, if you decide you are going to change all that, and begin the process of looking for joy within yourself. Give gratitude, accept the compliments when given, and share your thoughts with others in a positive manner, then you will be pleasantly surprised what has been right beside you all this time. Opportunities will now begin to present themselves, but if you do nothing to activate them and bring them to life in your world, then only you are the one to blame. If you find you are going in circles, then perhaps it time for you to change your direction, try something new and be open to whole new way of doing things. Change isn't always easy, and for some people it is very stressful, but then living a life that is not fulfilling or void of happiness, is not the best either. It comes down to making a choice; choosing to remain living in certainty or your comfort zone, which is really living in your past, or deciding to accept change into your life. You be the one to decide what that change will be, and in doing so create your future.

By now you will know that it isn't enough to simply say that things need to change. You have recognized whatever you are doing isn't working, so will the rest then be up the Universe to correct? It's not that easy. Recognizing you are tired of the way things are is one thing, and making up your mind to begin making a difference is another. Until you can honestly say, *"I am tired of feeling this way and I am willing and ready to change it, beginning right now",* nothing will happen. This is your journey, your choice. You need to be willing to make that commitment to seize the opportunities, ask for help, then be able to set your ego aside, and accept the help when it comes into your life. It is also about taking responsibility for your part in the whole situation, then without judgment or excuses admit you may have made a few mistakes, but having learned from them you are now going to forgive yourself and others, then learn and move forward with gratitude and love.

You may need to pick yourself up a few times, dust yourself off, and start again, but that is okay....you are on your way to making changes needed in your life. No one can do this for you...it is all up to you. Are you ready to begin your adventure, and step out of that comfort zone? Are you brave enough to ask the three soul questions, *Who am I? What do I desire? What is my purpose?* Are you able to trust that the answers will come to you when the time is right? Can you visualize yourself in a better place, emotionally, physically, and spiritually? You deserve and are worthy of joy, love, and compassion in your life. You are deserving of abundance in all areas of your life.

Think it, see it as though it already exists, feel it in every cell of your body, and above all, believe you have the power together with the Universe and the Divine, the desire, and the right to be all you can be. What are you waiting for? Now is the best time to awaken and let your spirit soar. Now is your time to *Make it Happen*!

About the Author

Rev. Janice Chrysler is an ordained Metaphysical Minister, Reiki Master, Certified Hypnotherapist, Intuitive Psychic Reader and author. She has designed, written and presented a variety of seminars which specialize in helping others on their road to self-discovery. Through her private Spiritual Coaching Sessions and group workshops she has assisted others in awakening spirituality in all aspects of their lives.

Rev. Janice has recorded several guided meditations as well she has created oracle cards all available through Mindful Journey. She can be booked for speaking or facilitating engagements when she is isn't busy performing Weddings, Namings and Celebration of Life services!

To learn more about Rev. Janice Chrysler and Mindful Journey visit:
www.mindfuljourney.ca
www.facebook.com/Mindful-Journey

Services by Rev. Janice Chrysler

Hypnosis Sessions:

- Spiritual Coaching
- Journey of the Soul

Workshops and Seminars

- Speaking engagements
- Full day or week long workshops and retreats

Intuitive Psychic Readings:

- In person
- Email
- Skype

Mindful Journey Publishing

- Make It Happen
- Beyond the Chakras Oracle Cards

Mindful Journey Meditation Series

- Beyond the Chakras Guided Meditation
- Just Relax
- Breathe
- Healing Lab
- Meeting Your Spirit Guide
- The Journey Has Begun
- Kids Can Meditate Too!
- Meditation For Teens
- Light, Love and Healing
- Lotus Flower